Marcel
Proust

Mary Ann Caws

D0003803

OVERLOOK DUCKWORTH

WOODSTOCK • NEW YORK • LONDON

First published in paperback in the United States in 2005 by
Overlook Duckworth, Peter Mayer Publishers, Inc.
New York, Woodstock, and London

NEW YORK:
141 Wooster Street
New York, NY 10012

WOODSTOCK:
One Overlook Drive
Woodstock, NY 12498
www.overlookpress.com
[For individual orders, bulk and special sales, contact our Woodstock office]

LONDON
Duckworth
90-93 Cowcross Street
London EC1M 6BF
www.ducknet.co.uk

Library of Congress Cataloging-in-Publication Data
Caws, Mary Ann.
Marcel Proust / Mary Ann Caws
p. cm.
Proust, Marcel, 1871-1922. 2. Novelists, French—20th century—Biography.
PQ2631.R63   Z545656   2003   2003054929

Type formatting and layout by Bernard Schleifer Company
Printed in Singapore
ISBN 1-58567-648-9
ISBN 0-7156-3256-6 (UK)
9 8 7 6 5 4 3 2 1

Contents

"This is the apparent life . . . the real life is underneath all this."

—*John Ruskin*, The Bible of Amiens[1]

Acknowledgments

The general enthusiasm surrounding anything to do with Proust is contagious. The way he appeals to what is not just public and largely readable – in whatever translation we have always loved or are newly attracted to – but to the private Proust many of us carry with us, makes a rare case for literature as a living entity.

My agent, Katherine Fausset, at Watkins Loomis, and my editors at Overlook, Tracy Carns and David Mulrooney, are greatly to be thanked, as are Robin Stolfi at Art Resource in New York, Agathe Colville at Roger-Viollet in Paris, Nathalie Bost-Ienn of the Centre des Monuments Nationeaux, Vincent Giroud of the Beinecke Library, Yale University, and Caroline Szylowicz and Madeline Gibson in the Rare Book and Special Collections, University of Illlinois Library.

Harold Augenbraum of the Mercantile Library was kind enough to invite me to give the Proust annual lecture that inspired much of the illustration in this volume, and to put the resources of the Mercantile Library to work with the Henri Peyre French Institute of the Graduate School, City University of New York, on the program of Proust and Film. Other presentations have helped me focus on what I wanted to do in this book: I remember speaking with the Proust Support Group in Los Angeles in particular. The piece I wrote for Elyane Dyzon-Jones and Inge Winner's MLA volume on *Teaching Proust* touches on many of the same issues of the visual/verbal interchange. My seminar at the Graduate School of CUNY on James, Proust, and Woolf, kept me at the task, as did, on the material side of things, the Research Foundation of CUNY, with a grant to help subsidize some of the images in this book.

This book is meant as both a salute to the private author each of us imagines, and the public one we can imagine together, looking through his eyes.

New York, May, 2003

Proust in overcoat, from Stephanie Huet, the Proust Comic Book

MARCEL PROUST

Prelude

If the great book about the quest of time lost still holds such
magnetism, it passes often by way of the caricatures of Proust in
bed, Proust and his madeleine, Proust and his heavy overcoat —
sometimes fur on the outside, sometimes inside — the coat
with a velvet collar, that collar always reaching his drooping dark
mustache under his melancholy dark-ringed eyes. On occasion,
the coat would open upon his evening suit, its sleeves ending at
his white gloves. . . . As the critic Edmund Wilson put it, with his
usual acumen, in 1930: "The little man with the great eyes, the
Saracen's beak and the ill-fitting dress shirt, still dominates his
and our own special contemporary world; he has supplied sym-
bols in terms of which we see it and in the light of which we may
better understand it. Let us not wonder, and let us not complain,
if he suffered from its most insidious diseases." Suffering and
disease aside, if the external details of Proust's life and appearance have so marked his eventual reception, there is likely to be
an intimate correspondence between these and his texts. Indeed,
I believe that there is.

The very exaggeration of detail and of personal appearance is
part of Proust's general and ever-increasing appeal. Malcolm
Bowie's *Proust Among the Stars* states categorically: "If Proust's
life had been in some respects mad, his novel was madder. . . ."
He continues with a link between Cabourg, in Normandy, and the
textual Balbec it became in the novel, invoking the sand and chilly

spray and "shingle of the Cabourg shore" as a prelude to the encounter with Proust's "gritty, breezy and salty book. . . ." Breezy is not the adjective I would most hastily reject for this present brief biography.

Given the celebrated biography of Marcel Proust by the insuperable writer who was George Painter, and more recently by those of Ronald Hayman, William Sansom, the brief and convincing one by Edmund White, the massive and authoritative work of William Carter, and the classically French approach of Jean-Yves Tadié, there is surely no need for a further massive tome. In this short volume, visually inclined, the images are given equal weight with the words. The approach emphasizes a few scenes, whose ideal presence would have something of the fragrance of hawthorn in the spring, and the muted resonance of Swann's sounding of the Sunday bell at the gate, "timid, oval, and gilded."

At the beginning, in view of its publication by Grasset, Proust described the idea of his work as he then saw it:

> At least it's from the novel form that it departs least. There is a person who narrates and who says "I"; there are a great many characters; they are "prepared" in this first volume, in such a way that in the second they will do exactly the opposite of what one would have expected from the first. From the publisher's point of view, unfortunately, the first volume is much less narrative than the second. And from the point of view of composition, it is so complex that it only becomes clear much later when all the "themes" have begun to coalesce.

That arrangement of complexity and coalescence holds also for Proust's life. Instead of the usual comforting outline stretching straight from cradle to coffin, Proust's life, beyond the banal clarity of madeleines and tea, society and salons, Céleste and coffee, combines, like his great work, the well-noted melancholy of memory with an ecstatic sensitivity to spectacle and a humor ranging from the quietly droll and the implicitly ironic to the side-splitting and outrageous.

Guiding Threads

Yes, his mother hovered over him ceaselessly, as his letters do over her. The celebrated scene of the goodnight kiss is based on life. Proust's letters to his mother are full of his longing to be by her side, forming yet again "one person as we are now one heart." The lovely and learned Jeanne Weil , married to the celebrated Dr. Adrien Proust, a specialist in cholera and other exotic diseases, would want to know every detail of the sicknesses and indispositions of her brilliant elder son. (Ah, Céleste, says Proust to his faithful housekeeper later, if only my work were to be as important as my father's . . .) And so it was to be.

A year after an early incident in the Champs-Élysées, on the first of May, 1880, in which he broke his nose, Proust's lifelong and serious asthmatic condition declared itself, so that he was in constant panic of suffocation, unable to breathe if certain conditions obtained, and ceaselessly conscious of living on the edge of the precipice. His brother Robert ("Proustovich" to his family), younger by two years and an object of both Marcel's love and his jealousy, was, like their mother, never far from his thoughts. Robert was, however, completely removed from the novel, and there are tales of his having, tit for tat, not delivered exactly the right text to the publishers after Proust's death at fifty-one.

One of the guiding threads of *In Search of Lost Time* (also known to readers of English as *Remembrance of Things Past*) is offered by the loving and brave grandmother, who has so many characteristics of his mother as well as of her mother, Grandmother Adèle Berncastel Weil, who in the novel loved to turn her face upward to the rain ("Ah, one can breathe!") and who was so devoted to authenticity of all sorts that she famously and heartily detested reproductions of anything at

Mme Adrien Proust, born Jeanne Weil (1849-1905).

Professeur Adrien Proust (1834-1903).

all. Mme Weil was a devotee of Mme de Sévigné, an excellent pianist, and as intimate with literature as Proust himself: she died, her daughter recounts, reciting passages from the playwrights Molière and Labiche. In the novel, her death inspires some of the most heartrending passages as well as the all-important theme of the "intermittences of the heart," those unaccountable and unpredictable emotions whose value resides precisely in their unexpected occurrence. She hides from her grandson her increasing sickness, making up her face so that it will not appear so stricken by illness. He notices only her over-cosmeticized appearance, and at her death, he does not grieve as he will later. If Marcel's mother went into deep mourning over her own mother, walking the beach in the rain with her face upturned in her honor, Marcel himself, apparently not grieving in the beginning, will be, two years later, suddenly overcome with ultimate distress one day as he bends over to tie his shoelaces. As the timing of anything in life is unpredictable, the time of deepest emotion is often not coincident with the event. The grief delayed is all the more terrible, and often accompanied by an equally terrible pang of conscience.

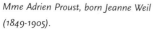

Marcel Proust (1871-1922), right, with his brother Robert.

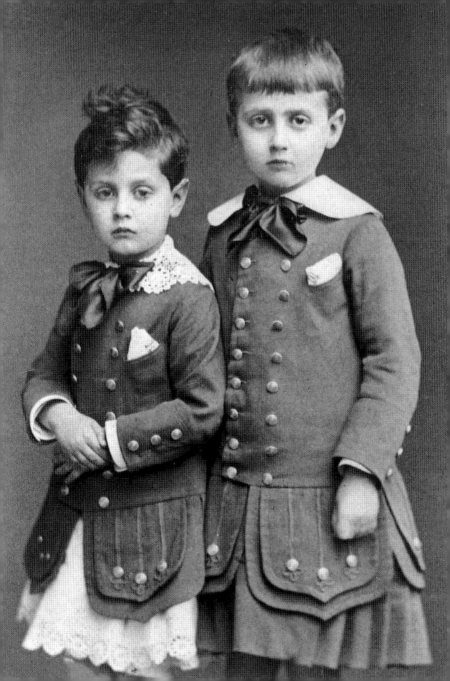

Entrance of the Lycée Condorcet, 65 rue Caumartin, IXème arrondissement, in 1913.

Tableau d'honneur (honor roll) in the Lycée Condorcet.

These intermittences of the heart gave one of the original titles for the entire novel, embracing the time lost and found, and its effect on the figures chosen to be embraced by it. Eventually, the search of the doubly significant time, both wasted and lost, took over. Because Francis Carco had used that title, *Le temps perdu*, Proust had to add the "*À la recherche*" introduction to it, and to make his way, in life and art, from the notion of wasted time to that of time lost: only the latter can be recaptured.

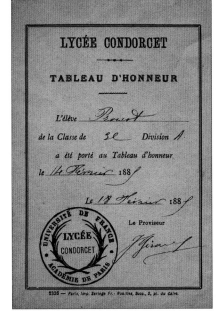

LYCÉE CONDORCET

TABLEAU D'HONNEUR

L'élève *Proust*

de la Classe de *3e* Division *A*

a été porté au Tableau d'honneur

le *14 Février* 188*

Le *18 Février* 188*

Le Proviseur

UNIVERSITÉ DE FRANCE
LYCÉE CONDORCET
ACADÉMIE DE PARIS

2336 — Paris, Imp. Seringe Fr.- Nœilles, Succ., 2, pl. du Caire.

His parents were both indulgent and thoughtful, in particular about Marcel's early education, supplying without question the substantial price of private lessons in philosophy and languages outside the regular courses of the Lycée Condorcet, many of which Proust missed because of his illnesses. About his extravagant ways and odd habits, they reprimanded him. Nevertheless, when one day, in anger over their reprimands, he smashed a delicate and handsome vase upon the floor, his mother wrote him that it was a symbol, as in a Jewish marriage when the glass is broken, not of breakage but rather of union. Please, she added, don't go barefooted into the room because the shards of glass would hurt your feet. She was endlessly solicitous of his feelings, a concern which was to mark his later relationships for better, and for worse.

Among Proust's most valued contacts were two of his professors. Alphonse Darlu, a brilliant teacher with a searching look, tutored him outside of school. It was in Darlu's class that he met Jacques Bizet, whose mother Mme Straus, widow of the composer Georges Bizet, remained a lifelong friend to Marcel and provided the meeting place for the schoolboy editors of the little and short-lived vaguely symbolist magazine *Le Banquet.* Subsequently, they edited *Le lundi* (Monday), *La Revue verte* (The Green Review), and *La Revue lilas* (The Lilac Review). Among the other young editors were the

Madame Straus (Geneviève Bizet) by Jules Élie Delaunay (1828-1891) The portrait was exhibited in the Salon of 1878, much admired by everyone except Degas, who found it artificial. After the composer Bizet died in 1875, Geneviève married the lawyer and art collector Émile Straus. Maupassant was madly in love with her, in vain. She was an enthusiastic reader of Proust.

The Viscount (then Marquis) Robert (Pellevé de la Motte-Ango) de Flers (1872-1927), ambasassor and then director of the Figaro and playwright of many "comédies de boulevard" written with Gaston de Caillavet, to whom Proust introduced him.

Viscount Robert de Flers, the Count Louis de la Salle, Fernand Gregh, Robert Dreyfus, Horace Finaly, and Daniel Halévy, Jacques Bizet's cousin, with whom Marcel was emotionally involved, founder of a movement he entitled "subtle-ism."

The other professor so important to him, Paul Desjardins, was the founder in 1892 of the nobly-titled L'Union pour la Vérité (Union for Truth), the precursor of the ten-day meetings (décades, modeled on Bocaccio's *Decameron*) at the Abbaye of Pontigny in Normandy, created in 1910. Gathered around Desjardins was the group of the *Nouvelle Revue Française*, including the theatre director Jacques Copeau and the writers Jacques Rivière and André Gide. Although Proust never finally attended any of the décades, and would have found his sleeping schedule ill fitted to the debates, he had clearly intended to. Having himself thought of establishing a com-

Paul Desjardins, founder of L'Union pour la Vérité and of the "décades" at Pontigny.

Madeleine Lemaire (1845-1928), Bouquet of Flowers.

munity of like-minded persons for such discussions, Proust was impressed with the entire enterprise, and once sent, by way of Rivière, his "homage to the Desjardins family: they are and will remain one of the dearest and most respected parts of the years I have lived."

Since his family could afford to help him buy his uniform, he was able to accomplish his military service in one year, as was the rule. His other brief occupations included, to please his father, training at both the École de Droit and the Institut des Études Politiques, at neither of which did he excel. Marcel tried to persuade his family that anything except philosophy and literature would be a waste of time for him, but did for a time occupy a position at the Bibliothèque Mazarine. The atmosphere, with all the books around, greatly appealed to him; nevertheless, his frequent absences and continual postponement of service finally led to his dismissal. From then on, his chief preoccupations were society and his writing. First he tried his hand at stories, those included in *Le Banquet*, which went to make up *Les Plaisirs et les jours* (Pleasures and Days). This work was originally entitled *Le Château de Réveillon*, after the home of his friend Madeleine Lemaire, a famous hostess, painter of roses, among other flowers, and the illustrator of the book. He also wrote a series of impressionist prose poems, as well as various reviews and columns for the papers, the longer and incomplete *Jean Santeuil*, preparatory for much of the great book of the *Search*, and the important essays in *Contre Sainte-Beuve*.

Early Place and Late

Of his family's dwelling on the boulevard Malesherbes, he remem-
bered the "honest smells of the soap and the wardrobe with its
mirror-glass doors" in the warm mornings. In the dining room,
"the air was transparent and congealed, like an immaterial agate
veined with the scent of the cherries already piled high in the fruit
dishes" and the little cut-glass knife rests, throwing "peacock-
feather patterns on the walls, which seemed to me as miraculous
as the stained-glass windows in the Reims Cathedral."

But it was in Illiers in Normandy, the home of his grandfather,
Louis Proust, and of his Aunt and Uncle Amiot, where his family spent
their vacation, that the goodnight kiss episode took place. The house
of "Tante Léonie," with its feeling of Sunday gossip and the taste of
the madeleine, feels familiar to all of us now. And it was a countryside
he felt with a child's intensity: "I could stay there for hours just looking
at the waters of the river Loire running by, then reading or writing in
the little pavilion with all of nature right under my eyes. . . ." and no
less with a grown-up nostalgia, permeating life and work. This was
Combray of the two paths or ways: "Villebon" and "Méséglise" (or
"Méréglise") as he first wrote them, developing into the bourgeois way
of Swann, and the noble way of the Guermantes. They seem opposed
in direction, until, much later in the novel and in time, they are seen to
converge, in the marriage of Gilberte Swann with the Guermantes family through Saint-Loup. They converge then on the map, psychologically
and personally. Proust's complexity of composition is seen to be an
organic whole, and more importantly, felt to be one. Proust senses
himself early on to have not just two ways of going, two paths of knowing, but a variety of choices and beings, himself multiple like Gabriele
d'Annunzio's hero in *The Intruder*, to whom he refers.

This sort of sensitivity offers both a caveat and a clue about the attempt to trace even the briefest biography of a self so multiple in its ways of knowing and being. I have chosen a non-linear approach, with the various directions taken in as free a manner as the novel itself and the life of reading it leads to.

Left: *The* Pré Catelan, *Uncle Amiot's garden. Surrounding this garden was a hedge of hawthorns, whose perfume is so powerful for the narrator of the* Search.
Below: *House of "Aunt Léonie," in Illiers.*

Above: Furniture of Marcel Proust, 102, boulevard Haussmann. December 1906 to June 1919.
Left: Réjane (1856-1920), French actress.

During his lifetime, Proust's frequent change of domicile occasioned a different disposal of his furniture — except for the piano and the three little tables with his medicines, his notebooks, and his coffee, and his bed. He was first in his family's apartment at 9, boulevard Malesherbes, then 45, rue de Courcelles, then 102, boulevard Haussmann, then, for four months, in the building of the actress Réjane and her son at 8 bis, rue Laurent-Pichat, in the small fourth-floor flat belonging to her daughter. Here the walls were so thin that the noise of lovemaking predominated over everything. Finally, he settled in a fifth-floor apartment at 44, rue Hamelin, where the daylight was shut out by floor-length blue satin curtains, the same color as in the Auteuil home of so long ago, completing a circle like that of the Time beginning and ending the long book.

But the essential address is his to us all. What he wanted to write was a book that we could take into our modest compartment on the train, a book that an electrician would pick up and be entranced by, a book that would not cost much. To that end, he himself contributed, not only by his non-stop writing efforts and his unforgettable characters, his overwhelming presence as a lyric and moving stylist, but his actual payment on his own volumes; his main concern was wanting to share his many ways with us.

During his movements here and there, in society and out, to all the cafés and restaurants he haunted, to Venice with its gilded domes of Saint Mark's Basilica and its lagoons, and to Cabourg by the sea — his Balbec — he never ceased gathering the material for his epic book. As Céleste, his housemaid and confidante of all the last years of his life said in her memoir: "Little Marcel always knew he would be the great Proust." He frequented an assortment of Paris cafés, like the Café Weber in the early years of the century, where Léon Daudet (the brother of the sweet-faced Lucien Daudet, one of Proust's first loves) described him in his *Salons et journaux* as "a pale, doe-eyed young man, sucking on or fingering the ends of his dark, drooping mustache, and swaddled in layers of wool like a Chinese curio." He was a familiar of no less an assortment of restaurants, particularly the grand and small dining rooms of Larue and the Ritz, where he would arrive late at night, ordering fresh vegetables, mashed

Top of the facade of the Basilica of Saint Mark, in Venice.

potatoes, and vanilla ice cream, and chatting with the endlessly knowledgeable Olivier Dabescat, the maître d', who was acquainted with all the latest gossip so essential to Proust the writer as a brilliant listener and talker, superbly rendering society's self-portrayal.

Marcel frequented various seasides: from Ostende, with the Finaly

Above: *Sarah Bernhardt (1844-1923), French actress, in Belle-Île (Morbihan, Brittany).*
Below: *Venice, gondolas on the lagoon, ca. 1900.*

family ("How good-looking and intelligent they are!" Proust wrote to Robert de Billy, a friend, in 1893), to the beach and the green waters of the Norman towns of Dieppe and Cabourg, the latter of major importance in the novel, where it becomes Balbec. He visited Beg-Meil in Brittany, and Belle-Île, reachable only by ferry, where he would like to have seen the home of Sarah Bernhardt and the rock where she liked to sit, but never did. To Cabourg he would return, and to the Venice painted by Whistler and Monet. Here he could see the paintings of his beloved Carpaccio, especially the St. Ursula sequence, precious to him because of John Ruskin's attachment to Venice and to that particular series, in which Ruskin situated the figure of his childlike love, Rose — a virgin like St. Ursula. Proust was particularly fascinated by the cloak worn by one of the Patriarchs of Grado — from which he was convinced that the fabric designer Fortuny had taken his design — so that the Narrator of Proust's novel will delight in bringing a Fortuny cloak to the shoulders of his mistress, the capricious and captive Albertine. Things and designs are wrapped in each other throughout the novel.

Right: *Dresses of Mariano Fortuny y Madrazo (1871-1949), with his famous pleats, worn by Lisa, Anna, and Margot Duncan, adopted daughters of Isadora Duncan, ca. 1920.*

Left: *Vittore Carpaccio (1455-1525), Legend of St. Ursula.*

Loves and Characters

Proust's loves were many, from early to late: some platonic and female, like the pretty and merry Marie de Benardaky in the park of the Champs-Élysées — the main contributor to the character of Gilberte with whom the Narrator plays, and like the lovely and cultivated Laure Hayman (later a sculptress), by whom he would stretch out on the bed. But always he preferred triangular relationships, extolling one friend or lover to the other, as he had Robert de Flers to Jacques Bizet, or Lucien Daudet to Daniel Halévy. There were was Louisa de Mornand and Louis d'Albufera, with each of whom he flirted in turn, as he did with Madame Straus and her son. Each of his loves seems to have lasted a little over a

year and a half, before giving way to the next. The hothouse atmosphere of his collaborative work and play is reflected in the famous picture by Otto of Proust, Daudet, and de Flers with his arm on Proust's shoulder, looking lovingly down at him. Proust's family detested this picture, with its none-too-subtle connotations. Of all Proust's lovers and close companions, the composer and singer Reynaldo Hahn

Marie de Benardaky

was no doubt the most loyal. Until Proust's death, he was never far away.

Proust had a period of intimacy with Prince Antoine Bibesco, who with his brother Emmanuel lived in a high-ceilinged house on the Île Saint-Louis, with tall Vuillard paintings reaching to the ceiling. The aristocratic features, blond hair, and blue eyes of Bertrand de Fénelon give Saint-Loup his distinction, although Jean Cocteau contributes also to his physical and mental aspects. Not all of Proust's lovers enter into the work: if his chauffeur Alfred Agostinelli gives some of his character to Albertine, her very imprisonment is no less inspired by the way in which one of Proust's last lovers, the waiter Henri Rochat, resided in the room near his own. The tall Scandinavian Ernest Forssgren was responsible for one of his last excursions to the outside world, when Proust went to wait for him in his hotel, in vain, before returning exhausted. What seems most inexhaustible is the profusion of figures composing the characters in this great novel, each of whom is based on multiple sources – as multiple as the styles and themes Proust offers us.

Proust's multiple selves reached out to others, to some lifelong companions, and to some relations fraught with tension, as with the older and mannered Count Robert de Montesquiou (called "the fatal count") on terms that were shifting at best. If Montesquiou is the main component of the larger than life Baron de Charlus, his tone and arrogance and mannerisms all serving the picture of that large figure — whose girth is far from his own thin elegance — the Baron is also the plump and highly

Count Robert de Montesquiou-Fezensac (1855-1921), French writer.

Jean Lorrain (1855-1906), French writer, far left; Jean-Louis Forain (1852-1931), French painter; fourth from the left; and, fifth from the left, the count Robert de Montesquiou-Fezensac.

unattractive Doäzen, perfumed, beringed, bejeweled, and what is worse, a close friend of the hateful Jean Lorrain, with whom Proust actually dueled. If the painter Elstir recalls in his name and genius Whistler, he has also aspects of Turner, as well as those of Paul Helleu, and the verbal tic of Vuillard. If the courtesan Odette de Crécy resembles Laure Hayman, she has also aspects of Louisa de Mornand. As for the incredible personage of Madame Verdurin, she shares the salon-making of Madeleine Lemaire and Madame de Caillavet (Madame Arman as she was called), as well as Madame Aubernon. The writer Bergotte reminds us of Ruskin and of Proust also, Albertine of Agostinelli, first his chauffeur and then his most adored lover.

And yet as our reading continues, and our acquaintance with Proust increases, the final recipe seems far more complex, and our enjoyment more sustained than parceled out. The sense of one organic entity, in all of Proustian writing at its finest, means that the location of the preface at the end of *Contre Sainte-Beuve* seems as logical as anything else: like Proust's discussion of Ruskin's "superior logic" that overarches and underlies all the reams of text. His own generosity seems to spread over the entire novel. "Be merciful," he quotes Ruskin as saying, "while you still have mercy." His novel inspires that feeling in the reader.

Joseph Mallord William Turner (1775-1851), Landscape with a River and a Bay in the Far Distance. *One of the rare Turners that Proust could have seen, in the collection of Camille Groult, where Edmond de Goncourt noticed it also. A perfect example of the novelist's merging of the earth and the sea, "one of the most frequent metaphors in the seascapes" of the painter Elstir.*

Reading

If Proust living and Proust writing were two entities, there were others. The theory of involuntary memory already required that. So, as he was reading or speaking, half of him would drift away, as Céleste recounts it. Suddenly, she said, he would be far removed: "this odd hesitation, as if half of him were continuing to talk while the other went off, and when it returned, it took a few minutes for them to join once more."

That is, we know, the way the imaginative mind works. Proust's essay "On Reading" of 1905 makes room for the reader's mind in what he elsewhere called, speaking of solitude and its gift, its "full, fruitful work on itself." The kind of companionship Proust offers us is "that pure and calm friendship reading is." For me, he wrote to Montesquiou, "reading means solitude." That he wanted to avoid being read to by this colorful and brilliantly longwinded friend was the origin of the statement, but it was, all the same, true. If Proust exceled in the ordinary forms of friendship — his excessive generosity underlining not just his desperate desire to be loved, as psychoanalysis would have it, but something exceptionally high-strung — he was particularly sensitive to the written text, his truest friend in the long run.

Although his own run was a mere fifty-one years, the extent of his work seems only to increase.

Poem by Proust: "Si le bleu de l'opale est tendre/ If the blue of the opal is tender..."

Si le bleu de l'opale est tendre
Est-ce d'aimer, confusément
Son clair de lune semble attendre
Un cœur qui saura le comprendre
La douceur de ciel bleu sourit au cœur aimant
Comme un pardon pour sa démence
Dans le ciel est-ce donc encore la nature qui
Jusqu'à ... ment
Est-ce déjà Dieu qui commence!
Si le bleu de vos ~~et triste~~ yeux est triste
~~Est-ce de n'aimer pas, d'aimer~~
Est-ce d'aimer ce qui n'existe
pas en ce monde. aimer est trop

~~Hélas~~ ~~vide et ton cœur si t~~
yeux pas
Tes yeux sont moins profonds que
n'est vide ton cœur
Le ciel est vide aussi jusqu'à ... profond

Tes yeux vagues, tes yeux arides
Tes yeux profonds tels ils sont vides
~~Vides et pas~~ profonds et vides sont
rien
Et la tendre de bleu pâle et
un mensonge dans l'opale
dans le ciel et...

Appearances

At first , we notice Proust as Colette describes him, in her *En pays connu*:

> "His extreme politeness, the excessive attention he paid to his
> interlocutors, especially if they were women, an attentiveness
> which emphazised the difference between them and him. He
> looked singularly young, younger than any of the men or any
> of the women. Large, melancholy, blackish-brown eye sockets,
> a complexion sometimes rosy and sometimes pale, anxious
> eyes, the mouth, when it was silent, tight and puckered, as if
> for a kiss, formal clothes and one intransigent lock of hair."

Colette is able to bring out, more perhaps than any other
observer of Proust's appearance, the excessive and the tragic in
his comportment. She sees him at the Ritz, where he for a while
thought of settling in as a resident. There she glimpses him surrounded by four or five friends, wearing his fur coat over his
evening suit and his cambric tie half unknotted:

> "He never stopped talking, trying to be gay. Because of the
> cold, and making excuses, he kept his top hat on, tilted back-
> wards, and the fan-like lock of hair covered his eyebrows. Full-
> dress uniform, but disarranged by a furious wind, which,
> pouring over the nape of his hat, rumpling the calico and the
> free ends of his cravat, filling in with a gray ash the furrows of
> his cheeks, the hollows of his eye sockets and the breathless
> mouth, had hunted this tottering young man of fifty to death."

A second description strikes a no less dramatic note, this
one by another in the same circle of society, the Marquis
de Clermont-Tonnerre:

*The writer Colette,
as a "little faun."*

"His pale thin face with a long aquiline nose, gave him an oriental appearance which became frankly Assyrian when he let his beard grow. Vast black pupils, which divulged no personal sentiment but looked like two receptacles ready to receive all the waves of space, let their orbs glisten round the interlocutors, and from the mouth which was often twisted by a one-sided smile came an extraordinary voice, rather puerile, caressing, pleasing, charged with a thousand gracious inflections, giving the impression of those little soft paws smeared with jam, which children put on your clothes, it is tender, sticky, you are both flattered and slightly irritated."

Much in the same vein is one of the young Proust's friends' remark about his general attitude: "To Proustify, we said, was to express a slightly too conscious attitude of geniality together with what would vulgarly have been called affectations, interminable and delicious."[2] In more complimentary terms, the Duchesse de Clermont-Tonnerre, formerly Élisabeth de Gramont, herself a writer and a lifelong friend of Proust, said of his work: "It's not a story whose end you want to rush to, but a miraculous walk leading from the earth to the heavens and descending to the depth of the oceans."

Left: *Élisabeth de Gramont, the Duchesse de Clermont-Tonnerre.*

Right: *Proust strumming on a tennis racket, before Jeanne Pouquet at the tennis court on the boulevard Bineau.*

All the Bloomsbury group: Virginia Woolf, Roger Fry, and the painter Carrington in particular, enthused about reading Proust. Woolf wrote to Fry in May 1922, after she had been asked to say a few words about him: "But Proust so titillates my own desire for expression that I can hardly set out the sentence. Oh if I could write like that! I cry. And at the moment such is the astonishing vibration and saturation and intensification that he procures — there's something sexual in it — that I feel I *can* write like that, and seize my pen and then I *can't* write like that. Scarcely anyone so stimulates the nerves of language in me: it becomes an obsession." And in October of the same year, "My great adventure is really Proust. Well — what remains to be written after that?. . . I am in a state of amazement. One has to put down the book and gasp." The writer and diplomat Harold Nicolson, arriving for the Peace Conference at the Quai d'Orsay describes the man who fascinated him, in spite of his pallid and grubby appearance, "he would put on his elaborate evening clothes (those white kid gloves clasping an opera hat) and attend the receptions given to members of the Peace Conference. He appeared there like Beethoven at the Congress of Vienna . . . unaware of the early and enduring monument of his own impending fame."

Proust, sometimes called handsome and sometimes Oriental, and often accused of a fawning demeanor, could make fun of his own appearance. Writing to Bertrand de Fénelon, he recounts the reaction of the Duc de Gramont when he was to sign a visitor's book, and "filled with anxiety by my humble and confused demeanor," asked him to write his name but "no thoughts." Much more appropriate, says Proust, if I had been addressing him that way.

The writer Jacques-Émile Blanche — whose father, a psychiatrist, had his private lunatic asylum at Autueil, with Guy de Maupassant as one of the inmates —had studied English under Mallarmé and was a close friend of the Bloomsbury group. He made the most famous portrait of Proust, who wrote a preface to his book *Propos de peintre: de David à Degas*, asking that he be allowed to mention therein Vuillard, Denis, and Picasso, all of whom he admired unstintingly.

Marcel Proust by Jacques-Émile Blanche, the famous portrait.

According to some recountings, Blanche, understandably uncomfortable with the image he had made of this tight-lipped fop, tore up the painting, of which Proust rescued just the visage and upper torso, preserving the catleya flower, or then the orchid in his pocket, symbolic of the famous scenes in which Swann makes love with Odette. Proust, however, in other versions of the story, kept the portrait, which some find highly displeasing.

As for his vestimental appearance, in the early part of his life, Proust would more likely than not wear a tie of palest green, a floppy jacket with large shirts, and baggy trousers. Later, when he decided to dress with more care, he would spare no expense, extravagant in this as in most things: a large tipper, an inveterate present-giver, a bestower of immense bouquets, he would dress himself from the ultra-chic Carnaval de Venise, at the corner of the rue des Capucines and the rue Scribe, not far from the Opera. He had suits in somber colors, with buttoned boots, over which his black socks would occasionally droop, to his complete unconcern. He would have private fittings in his apartment for his dress suit, a jacket with striped trousers, a black vest and bowtie, and a suit with tails and white tie. He even had a waistcoat of red silk, lined with white silk. Proust greatly admired Boni de Castellane, impoverished man about town and giver of great dinners, who could always tell you where to buy some expensive gifts at half price. Proust would marvel at his getup, and his elegant eccentricity "like a handsome bulldog with his copper collar that looks so much like gold. Well, he doesn't have a penny!" When you think, he exclaimed to Céleste, that those people sleep on the edge of a bathtub, but what an appearance they keep up! His own appearance he cared about, with a certain downplaying of his way of dressing: When Proust went out of town, to the seaside at Cabourg ("Queen of the Beaches"), he would take two overcoats, one in brown vicuna, and the other, in a grayish-white plaid with a violet lining, he would hang so the color of the lining would not be noticeable.

This is reminiscent of his embarrassment when young over being invited to the grand balls, about which he would hide the truth, as he would in the train, when he had a first-class ticket but

The Grand Hotel, in Cabourg (Calvados), ca. 1900.

rode with his friends in third-class. He returned often to the Grand Hotel at Cabourg, to the delight of the hotel staff, where the personnel well knew his habit of tipping generously, and of the crowd of young girls gathered around the baccarat table in the casino, with whom he was no less a favorite than with the hotel staff.

But when he was older, Proust was not just a great admirer of appearances, and of those who kept them up, but a great envier of luxury. He much admired the fact that the Countess Greffulhe had at least forty servants. He cared what he had with him, and frequently lost it, a trait endearingly careless. As Jacques-Émile Blanche describes it:

> "He carried a malacca cane which he had a way of twirling whenever he stooped to pick up a dropped glove (his gloves were pearl gray with black stitching, and were always crumpled and dirty), or was engaged in putting on or taking off its fellow. He was forever leaving odd gloves about, or would implore their return by post, in exchange for a new pair, or for

half a dozen new pairs, which he liked to present as a thank you to whomever would be kind enough to find his strays for him. The same thing was constantly happening to his umbrellas, which he left in cabs or in the halls of his friends' houses. No matter how dilapidated they might be, he continued to use them when his appeal for their return was answered, though he invariably bought the friend in question a new one at Verdier's. His top hats very soon took on the appearance of hedgehogs or Skye terriers, as a result of being brushed the wrong way, or rubbed against the skirts or furs of his driving companions."

Proust's neurasthenia is well-documented and, depending on one's reactions, hilarious or moving — or both. As for the grander moments, at the moment when Robert was to marry Marthe in the nearby church of St. Augustin, Proust, panicked as usual over the notion that he might be cold, stuffed his tuxedo with a great mass of thermal wadding, placed several mufflers around his neck, and three overcoats over the tux, and so attired, was too massive to get down the aisle and had to stand aside. "To each row in turn he announced in a loud voice that he was not able to dress otherwise, that he had been ill for months, that he would be still more ill that evening, that it was not his fault."

In some humbler moments previous to this, he would fasten a particular safety pin to his underpants, believing this to be efficacious against tummyaches. So he writes his mother of his desire to share her normal schedule of sleeping and waking but of the obstacles thereto: "I couldn't find my safety pin (the one I use to close and tighten my drawers. Naturally, the night was over for me, there was nothing to hold my stomach." Unable to find in her dressing room a suitable pin, he was deprived of rest. His sleeping arrangements and his comfort in bed, were, like the coffee which sustained him waking, a more than essential concern: an obsession. When, in his increasing invalidism at the end of his life, he was spending the major part of his time in bed, he would wear a baggy sweater and long johns of Rasurel wool, purchased

Fragment of a Proust manuscript, "Comme on se promène au bord de la mer" (As we walk along the seashore).

in the same store on the Boulevard Haussmann — clothing that would breathe, as he often could not. Like the water, everything that touched him had to be of exactly his temperature: his sweaters, shorts, and shirts, so Céleste would keep them warmed and ready in the kitchen, by the brick oven, wrapped in terrycloth, and then upon his chair. He would get up in his pajama top, with his sweater from the Pyrenees and his long johns, put on his overcoat with its black and white squares, change his bedhose for *babouches* or slippers in heavy cloth, and never shave unless he was going out.

Receiving visitors in bed was a crucial part of his existence: he never wanted a woman to come to his bedside. This rule was infringed only once, when Prince Antoine Bibesco sneaked his fiancée in by carrying her in his arms behind Céleste, so eager was she to see the famous author in his habitual position.

Daily Life

In his morning (he slept from eight A.M. to three P.M., so the term is relative), Proust would take his croissant from a patissier in the rue de la Pépinière with his café au lait — the milk always freshly boiled — having in reserve another in his saucer. The coffee pot with his initials on it held two cups, from which he took exactly one and a half cups at first, filling the gilt-edged bowl to the top with the milk. For the second bowl, which he would take directly after the other, the milk had to be freshly boiled once more. With his croissant, he liked jam; it would have to come from Tanrade, on the rue de Sèze, behind the Madeleine.

Everything about his diet was specific. The ingredients came from his favorite places, his care for detail being as great about this as in his novel. He would like his *boeuf à la mode* made by Félicie, in its jelly and with a few carrots, or a fresh fish from his favourite fishmonger, Felix Potin, on the place Saint-Augustin, fried to perfection, served on a large porcelain plate, on a damask napkin folded in two, with a half-lemon on each of the four corners. Or then he might prefer a *petite marmite*, made of beef, chicken gizzards, and other things, simmered together, and prepared by his favorite restaurant, Chez Larue, or perhaps a few of their *éperlans,* with scrambled eggs and Russian salad. He might order *rougets* from Prunier, the classic fish restaurant. Marcel was enormously fond of Rebattet's *petits fours,* of raspberry and strawberry ice cream from the Ritz, particularly when he arrived home late, and of anything chocolate from Latinbille, on the rue La Boétie, that mercifully stayed open for long hours. He would order his pears or grapes from Auger on the Boulevard Haussmann.

Proust disliked red wine, but liked "every white wine in the world, beer, cider. . . ." He also liked Contrexville or Evian water. Toward the end of his life, although he might at times eat copiously, he subsisted mainly on coffee. The thought that the two giants of French literature, Balzac and Proust, survived so long and brilliantly on so very many cups of coffee — Proust would have between six and twelve small cups of the strongest variety after dinner — is a matter of marvel to all their readers.

Restaurant Larue, Paris, in 1938.

Multiple Loves and Worlds

From the beginning, the young men, and occasionally women, with whom Marcel Proust chose to associate with were the most attractive, or certainly the most noticeable, often glamorous. As Proust said in his communications with his various beloveds over the years — and they were many — his interests in the body and in the mind were closely related.

There were beings caricatured and just as convincing as the others. The drolly mannered Madame Verdurin (based on Madame Georges Aubernon and her literary and artistic salon, where Proust met Robert de Montesquiou, and where he would often go with Reynaldo Hahn and the painter Jacques-Émile Blanche) and the extraordinary Baron de Charlus (based on Montesquiou) would

belong to the former category. More admirable were Bertrand de Fénelon, the major component of the blond, blue-eyed, aristocratic, and "bimetallic" (bisexual) Saint-Loup, along with Armand, Duc de Guiche, a painter, scientist, and enduring friend (whose half-sister was Élisabeth de Gramont), and the Countess de Greffulhe, born as the Princess Élisabeth de Caraman-Chimay, well aware of her stunning beauty, and one of the main sources for the

Madame Georges Aubernon.

The Countess Greffulhe (the Princess Élisabeth de Caraman-Chimay), in a black velvet dress embroidered with pearls and silver lillies. Proust met her in 1894, at the house of Robert de Montesquiou, her cousin. She was the primary model for the Duchesse de Guermantes, with her self-love and unhappy marriage.

Laure Hayman.

Duchesse de Guermantes. In the words of Élisabeth de Gramont, this Countess never "displayed herself to the crowd except from the top of a staircase, or surrounded by kings." Modestly, she said of herself, to the equally immodest Robert de Montesquiou, "I have only been understood by you . . . and the sun!" In every picture of either of them, the pose is studied and self-glorifying.

Proust's various amatory interests began with his early attractions to the tall blonde Marie de Benardaky, the original model for Gilberte whom he met in the park and would eagerly go to encounter every day, and to the various elegant light ladies like Laure Hayman, one of the many mistresses of his Uncle Louis at Auteuil, who, like Louisa de Mornand, was one of the components of Odette de Crécy. Proust's flirtation with her extended further than with many of the ladies to whom he paid tribute and court. At the death of Uncle Louis, whose family had expressly asked no flowers be sent, a delivery boy on a bicycle arrived at the end of the service with an enormous wreath: Laure had not wanted to raise eyebrows by coming herself. Then there was Daniel Halévy, one of his first associations at school, to whom Marcel wrote as a soulmate: "My moral principles allow me to believe the pleasures of the senses are good. . . . If you are delicious, if you have pretty bright eyes which reflect the fine delicacy of your mind so purely that I feel I cannot love your mind fully unless I kiss your eyes . . . if, finally, I feel that the charm of your self, your self in which I can't separate your lively mind from your lithe body . . ." and the rest is easily imagined. The series of "if"s were as honest as they were self-justifying.

As already mentioned, Halévy's mother, Geneviève Straus, had been the wife of Georges Bizet, before marrying Emile Straus, whose half-closed eyes and great crease in his forehead, added to a certain anti-Semitism characteristic of French society in that epoch, did not make him deeply loved. Marrying him was the only way of getting rid of him, said the witty Geneviève. They moved to a large townhouse at 134, boulevard Haussmann, near the Proust family, where Mme Straus held her celebrated Saturday salons. The memory of a red dress and matching shoes he had seen her wearing years before was his inspiration for the terrible passage that concludes *The Guermantes Way*, about the Duchesse de Guermantes and her red shoes, more important to the Duke and herself than Swann's announcement of his illness. (She had started out wearing the wrong color of shoes for her dress: unforgivable.) It

was at Mme Straus's that Proust met so many of the artists and writers who would be essential to him, like Gabriel Fauré, Edgar Degas, Sarah Bernhardt, as well as society figures like the redheaded aristocrat Charles Haas, the original of Swann, a member of the Cercle de la Rue

Sarah Bernhardt (1844-1923), French actress. This painting by Georges Clairin (1843-1919) hung in Bernhardt's salon on the boulevard Pereire. Proust met Clairin, a society painter and student of the Orient, in Madeleine Lemaire's salon.

Charles Haas.

Elegant fashion at the grand prix of the Jockey Club in Chantilly, 1909.

Royale, a close friend of the Prince of Wales and of many artists and writers, a connoisseur of Italian painting and of the Enlightenment, and the only Jewish member of the more than exclusive Jockey Club.

Then there was the closest friend he had in his lifetime, the enormously charming and talented composer and musician Reynaldo Hahn, Jewish-Catholic like Proust, born in Venezuela and a prodigy at the Paris Conservatoire, later a celebrated composer and conductor. ("Everything I've ever done is always 'thanks to Reynaldo,'" Proust declared at one point.[3] They corresponded in a kind of jargon, adding the consonants "ch" and "h" here and there, using private words like "mosch" or "moschant" for bad or "mechant" with homosexual overtones, referring to each other as "Salaistes" or spelling names backwards or with anagrammatic nicknames, as Proust to Reynaldo, "Binibuls,"

"Buncht," "Guncht," and "Birnechnibus" (visible in many of Proust's drawings), or Proust calling Antoine Bibesco "Oscebib" or "Bourbesco," calling Fénelon "Nonelef." In like manner, to his friends Proust became "Lecram" or then "Stroup," and so on. The delight of coding added to the drama of sexuality. Lucien Daudet, who replaced Reynaldo in Proust's physical affections, was especially gifted at imitation and could be called upon to "do a Zola," for example, so that he would look at the golden light above the Madeleine church and exclaim how over all of worka-day "Parith toppled thwateth of thultry radianthe," and so on. In the long run, most of Proust's lovers made, in their continuing

Reynaldo Hahn.

Oscar Wilde (1854-1900), Irish writer

friendship with him, a kind of peace with their amatory interests.

Proust's frequent encounters with other "Salaists" or "Saturniens" or inverts were given a particular spice by the social need, still in that period, of covering up what was sometimes referred to as "the German vice." It may be that Proust's notable flirtations with various females were useful also in that sense. One of the more delightful confrontations or semi-meetings took place with Oscar Wilde. The famous corpulent wit was invited to dine in the apartment of the Boulevard Haussmann, but the host arrived with five minutes delay only to be told that Monsieur Wilde was closeted in the toilet. Proust dashed in that direction and inquired, in his improbably sweet and childlike voice: "Monsieur Wilde, are you ill?" "Ah," replied the voice from the lavatory, "there you are, Monsieur Proust. No, I am not in the least ill. I thought I was to have the pleasure of dining with you alone, but when they showed me into the drawing room and at the end of the drawing room were your parents, my courage failed me. Goodbye, Monsieur Proust, goodbye." Wilde's *Salomé* (in French) — the heroine of a triumphantly baroque imagination as Gustave Moreau pictures her in *The Apparition* — was an instant success in Paris and enthusiastically reviewed by Montesquiou in *Le Figaro*, to whose editor, Gaston Calmette, *Du côté de chez Swann* was dedicated in 1913, when Grasset published it.

André Gide, famously sharing, like Jean Cocteau, Proust's friendship and his sexual inclinations, went to sit at Proust's bedside late one

Gustave Moreau (1826-1898), The Apparition, *ca. 1876, which hangs on the wall of the narrator's room in* Jean Santeuil. *Proust often uses the word "apparition" associated with this painter.*

night. They had become friends, even after Gide had so rapidly turned down for Gallimard Proust's manuscript, having read, as he later courageously confessed to the author, only two passages, having believed him to be simply a society fop, an amateur writer. This was the worst mistake he and the *Nouvelle Revue Français* had ever made, he gallantly said, and for the rest of his life he endeavored to promote Proust's work. He helped rescue the masterwork from the publishers during the war,

Above: Gaston Calmette.

Right: Letter from Marcel Proust to Gaston Calmette

when paper was scarce and publication slow. He finally managed to find a privileged niche for it at France's main publishing house, Editions Gallimard, defended it there, and helped see to its being awarded various prizes. When Gide read excerpts in the *NRF*, he exclaimed that he was enchanted: "through the strange and powerful subtlety of your style I seem to be reading . . . my own memories and my most personal sensations." And Gide

continued, in a column for the *NRF*, about Proust's style, that it was "so disconcerting in its suppleness that any other style appears stilted, dull, imprecise, sketchy, lifeless." After its richness, he said, his own felt like poverty itself.

For a time, Proust maintained the package delivered to Gallimard had not been opened, perhaps to preserve his own pride; in any case, he and Gide became friends, to the point, years later, of discussing with each other their sexual habits and ideas. What Proust told Gide, according to the latter, throws some light on one of the most troubling of Proust's customs.

It is well-known that for the needs of his novel, Proust would summon the keepers of records of various male brothels, so that they could brief him on their case histories of flagellants — necessary for the tale of Charlus and the go-between Morel. Even the name of Charlus was taken from that of a vaudeville singer working in such a brothel, while his voice was modeled after the preposterous Montesquiou, and his bloated body after the Baron Albert-Agapit Doäzan, from whom Montesquiou had pirated his secretary and inseparable companion, the no less preposterous Gabriel d'Yturri. Proust befriended the shifty Albert Le Cuziat, who seemed, for all his detailed knowledge of families and the intimate preferences of their members, to be some sort of living Almanach de Gotha. To his unsavory place, Proust not only contributed money and furniture, upon the occasion of moving apartments, but often went. As in the haunts in the small, dark streets of Venice that he and others like Henry James would frequent, customers had their favorite habits.

Proust would watch through the window where a few boys would be playing cards, and would choose one. The young man would then be summoned to the room where the author would be lying in bed, sheeted to his chin, and would have to take off his clothes and masturbate, while Proust would do the same. On the occasions when he was not successful, he would call for Le Cuziat to bring to his bed two cages, each with a starving rat. They would be let loose at each other, or, alternatively, would be pricked with pins. Proust, said Gide, explained this to him as "his preoccupation with combining, for the sake of orgasm, the most heterogeneous sensations and emotions."

Montesquiou, Whistler, and Various Outlandish Characters

Of all the remarkable characters whom Proust frequented in real life and used for his fictional creations — generally made up of several acquaintances, each of whom would lend his or her attributes to a panoply of figures — the one winning hands down was "the fatal count," Robert de Montesquiou. With his rouged cheeks, his wavy thick black hair and mustache and his tiny teeth, no less black, that he would hide behind a dainty hand when he laughed, with his pink Liberty cravat and green waistcoat, Grotesquiou or Hortensiou (so called for his poems on his favorite flower, the Blue Hortensia — *Les Hortensias bleues*) modelled his fluted voice and pose on those of his idol, the incredibly arrogant and no less brilliant Scottish-American painter, James Abbott McNeill Whistler. To the latter, Edgar Degas,

James Abbott McNeill Whistler, (1834-1903) Harmony in Blue and Silver: Trouville, 1845.

no bundle of easygoingness himself, had once remarked: "If you weren't such a genius, you would be the most impossible figure in London." Or, of course, in Paris. In Whistler's celebrated portrait of Montesquiou, which once hung in Montesquiou's home, he is carrying the chinchilla cloak of the Countess Greffulhe, because he wanted something of hers in the picture.

The immense impact of Whistler's character and his pose, more even than his unquestioned genius — his signature white splash of hair against the black and his signature butterfly — was out of all proportion to his diminutive size. Whistler's aesthetic manifesto of artistic privilege beyond and separate from morality, called the Ten O'clock (because he delivered it at ten P.M., after the audience would have dined in London) was translated into French by Whistler's great friend, the symbolist poet Mallarmé, with the help of the American Viélé-Griffin and the Irishman George Moore. Whistler lived at 110, rue du Bac, where he exhibited his collection of Chinese porcelain in blue and white, and entertained at breakfast. He appeared as part of the group of French impressionist painters in Fantin-Latour's celebrated group portrait. "Reserve me a good place," he had wired the painter.

Count Robert de Montsquiou, "the fatal count," by Whistler.

"Oscar is coming! Hide the silver!" Whistler had once warned his friend Mallarmé, who then wrote him, in his customary kindness, of how much he, Whistler, had been missed. Proust, as fascinated by Whistler as was Montesquiou, kept a photograph of Whistler's portrait of Carlyle in his bedroom, "my intentionally naked room," as he wrote to Marie Nordlinger. She was a young bilingual English artist and his major helper in the translation of Ruskin (after his beloved and learned mother had done a literal rendering for

him), with the occasional help of Robert, Vicomte d'Humières (the translator of Kipling, an author whose knowledge of wild beasts and the adventures associated with them fascinated Proust). Of the picture, Proust wrote that Carlyle's "serpentine overcoat" resembled Whistler's mother's dress in the more celebrated 1905 portrait, and sent a caricature of it to Reynaldo.

Left: Whistler's Arrangement in Grey and Black No. 2, or the Artist's Mother (Anna Mathilda McNeill, 1804-81), *1871.*

Proust's relations with Montesquiou, whom he originally admired immensely and flattered accordingly, were often troubled. The Fatal Count was himself quite a troubler, having among his other delightful habits that of going around to various salons and saying to each hostess how very ugly their guests looked that evening. At his performative best, he was fond of gesticulating with his white gloves and without. All of a sudden, he would point heavenward, his voice rising "like a trumpet in an orchestra," and passing into a high loud soprano, he would stamp his foot, toss back his head, and emit loud peals of "shrill, maniacal laughter." Proust could, and did one late Parisian night, imitate his "piercing cries" and gestures, at the house of Alphonse Daudet. Word of this somehow got back to the Count, who thereupon accused Proust of being "the traveling salesman of his wit." Wounded (and embarrassed), Proust answered him (December 12, 1895) that since "the body follows the soul," his voice and accent "may well have taken on the rhythm of this borrowed thought" which he so admired in any case. Proust's most admired gesture for Montesquiou was to introduce him to the young angelic-looking musician Léon Delafosse, with whom Montesquiou was infatuated for three years. After he tired of him, the angel (but from the ditch, "de la fosse") became just another "œuf brouillé" (scrambled egg, playing on the word *brouille* or quarrel.) Much of Delafosse is recognizable in the character of Charles Morel.

In the 1920s, Montesquiou went on a lecture trip to the United States, sponsored by Bessie Marbury — an American friend of the socialite and eternally impoverished and no less elegant Boni de Castellane — who lived with Miss Elsie de Wolfe (Lady Mendl). Writing him in his exaggerated and flattering manner, Proust compared the older writer and his improbable and inseparable Basque manservant Yturri to Saint Paul and Timothy on their epic evangelical stint for the deprived populations of the New World. He would parody, and in so doing, celebrate Montesquiou's parties ("Une Fête chez Montesquiou à Neuilly") in the well-circulated *Le Figaro* under the pseudonym "Horatio" and suffered a bout of acute embarrassment when Montesquiou questioned him about

The Marquis Boni (Boniface) de Castellane(1867-1932). Once enormously rich through the fortune of his wife, the American heiress Anna Gould, he became impoverished at their divorce, but had time to build his "rose palace" on the avenue du Bois.

the identity of the author. However, Montesquiou's vanity triumphed, and he would eventually have the article bound as a pamphlet in his own honor.

Montesquiou's poems were called by titles such as "Les Perles rouges" ("The Red Pearls"), "Le Chef des odeurs suaves," ("The commander of superb odors") and worse. Montesquiou held his salon and his poetry readings (generally of his own works: "Have you ever *heard* anything more wonderful," he would exclaim to whomever would listen) at his home in Versailles, first the *Pavillon Montesquiou*, then another, in Neuilly, delicately called *Le Palais des Muses*, where, in the spring, he would receive his friends between four and seven on Thursdays. Whistler's portrait of him graced the dining room, while Boldini's was none too subtly placed on a easel in what he called the White Salon.

Bisexual, Montesquiou is sup-

Giovanni Boldini (1845-1931), Count Robert de Montesquiou, *1897.*

Above: *Sarah Bernhardt in Racine's* Phèdre.

Below: *Anna de Noailles (1876-1933).*

posed to have thrown up for a week after making love to Sarah Bernhardt ("the divine Sarah," who, with Réjane, was the source figure for La Berma, Marcel's beloved actress). She came to his Palace at Proust's behest to recite the bejeweled lyrics of the renowned, short, and bright-eyed Anna de Noailles: about one of her stories, Montesquiou exclaimed, "from all the height of my infallible taste, and all the breadth of my infinite culture, I can say it is the most beautiful thing that has ever been written! . . . What genius! What genius!" And then he would repeat the entire story by heart again. It was through Montesquiou, briefly one of Proust's idols, that he was invited to many salons, including those of the Duchesse de Gramont and her sister, the Princess de Wagram. A friend of many of his more wordly friends, like Mme de Clermont-Tonnerre, whom Proust interrogated at length when he was writing his *Sodom and Gomorrah* chapter, Natalie Barney, author of the *Penseés d'une amazone* (Thoughts of an Amazon) wrote him to say that his book "was ravishing and profound and puts mine to shame." Although they made plans to meet, they never did. Barney's receptions on the rue Jacob, home of her "Temple d'Amitié," were frequented

Natalie Clifford Barney (1876-1972), American writer, standing in front of a tapestry given her by Count Robert de Montesquiou, ca. 1925-1930.

by Paris's most interesting writers, artists, and celebrated persons, including her lovers Djuna Barnes and Romaine Brooks, as well as Gertrude Stein, the Duchesse de Clermont-Tonnerre and many others. Barney's relation to the actress and well-known beauty Liane de Pougy (also known as a "courtesan," in all the good and bad senses of the term) had lasted for years, and the lesbian circles in Paris fascinated Proust.

Liane felt she had to defend Barney's relations. Although she herself disliked Pauline Tarn (whose pseudonym was Renée Vivien), she explained: "dung is necessary to the blooming of lilies . . . perhaps Pauline's genius was so admirable and special precisely because she had

Liane de Pougy (1869-1963), French courtesan and actress.

Poster for Jean Lorrain and Ed. Diet, "Rêve de Noël," performed by Liane de Pougy and Rose Demay at the Olympia, in December 1896, in Paris.

given free rein to the materiality of her earthly envelope." For Liane, Natalie remained "the Exquisite, the Incomparable in spite of having allowed every kind of touch." And even when their affair had died down long since, she retained the excitement of the first love. Here are a few entries: "My Flossie came to see me . . . She was dressed jauntily — Amazon style, what else! In a dark wool dress lightened by a green-embroidered white waistcoat. A caped coat over her shoulders, a plain felt hat on her blonde hair. With her brisk style, her implacable smile, her tenderness towards me, her instinctively caressing little hands, she looked very young and very happy."

And again: "Flossie was putty-colored from head to foot, complexion, teeth and hair included, and delicious and affection-ate . . . I love seeing Flossie again, listening to her, watching her make her way through the world of her choice — easily the most charming of worlds. And she enjoys returning to me from time to time. To some extent I am her creation. Although she is younger than I am, she was my exquisite teacher and opened horizons to me." Finally, and later, in her room: "Flossie came and lay down beside me. . . . I committed the delicious sin of abandoning myself to her caressing hands . . . N. and I were laughing like children at nothing and everything and it was infectious."

The feeling in the lesbian and homosexual circles is much the same: delicious indeed, slightly mannered, and often with an edge of humorous cruelty, especially toward the other sex. Liane describes a scene at her house between Cocteau and the painter and poet Max Jacob, a flagrantly mannered Jewish convert to Catholicism who would eventually die at Drancy, the halfway house to the concentration camps. She had put a vase of dahlias in the middle of the table, yellow, red, and orange. "'I can't see Max because of the flowers.' — 'I can't see Jean because of the flowers' — 'Well, what of it? You don't have to see each other'— 'Yes, we do' — 'Yes we do' — 'Too bad, there's no solution.' — 'Take away the flowers, Liane, they must go . . .' and Cocteau reached out for them."

Montesquiou, given to writing poems and delivering lectures, would send the exhausted Yturri to summon Proust to attend them, with no sensitivity to the asthmatic author's sleeping schedule, even "in the small hours of the afternoon." (Allergic to the sun's rays, Proust would sleep from eight in the morning until three in the afternoon, in spite of his mother's imploring him to adopt a more conventional arrangement). When once Proust did not appear for a Montesquiou reading — "On Fragments of Hugo's Fin de Satan," on April 21, 1905, in the Theatre Bouffes — the poet took revenge by forcing himself upon the novelist with a seven-hour stint of brilliant monologue and a reading of essays and poems at his bedside. Exhausting, said Proust, recognizing the brilliance but regretting those seven hours. Occasionally, Proust was supposed to invite an audience for such readings, and did so with a great deal of initial reluctance, comparing Montesquiou to Gustave Moreau's gigantic *Jupiter*, "always taking the leading role." Montesquiou responded that there was no need to take a role of which he was already assured. Perhaps in arranging the company for a reading by Montesquiou of his latest poems, they could work as partners, queried the poet? But Proust, accustomed to managing everything about his dinners: from the food and the seating (to

Mme Straus, "come early or I will have to seat you badly") to the costumes, retorted:

> "I attach importance to lounge suits, which makes it possible for me to invite one or two more friends without making a dinner of it, which I want to avoid at all costs. Ask your cousin Chimay to come to dinner on Wednesday in a high-necked dress or a house gown."

He needed to see the exact detail of her costume for his novel, and seldom lost an occasion to learn something from someone.

Proust would also arrange readings, such as those of the poems of Anna de Noailles read by the Divine Sarah in Madeleine Lemaire's glass-roofed studio. Known for her musical and literary Tuesday evenings, and for her paintings of flowers, the hostess would be found painting roses when her guests arrived, and just put down her brush, wanting the illusion of a painter who has guests rather than a society hostess who paints on the side. "She must have created more roses than anyone except God," it is said of Mme de Villeparisis in the novel. She was, along with Mme de

Caillavet — Anatole France's plump mistress, who entertained on Sundays — the main source of the unforgettable Madame Verdurin. There were, in her entertainments, the "faithful" who returned and the "infidels" who strayed . . . Proust knew when to be faithful.

Sarah Bernhardt, by Paul Nadar.

Ruskin and Others

Proust had every reason for his initial enthusiasm for the English genius, the writer, botanist, artist, and aesthetician John Ruskin. In his exclusive focus — nothing with him bore fruit unless it began as an obsession — he planned at length and finally executed a trip to Italy to see it through the older man's eyes. Ruskin's intensity of vision was never grasped more accurately by any writer than by Proust, and never communicated more vividly to anyone than to him. Proust spent endless hours in the *Bibliothèque Nationale* reading *The Seven Lamps of Architecture*, having already encountered Robert de la Sizeranne's seminal book on *Ruskin and the Religion of Beauty*, and excerpts of Ruskin's works in a review to which he subscribed, edited by his teacher Paul Desjardins. At Ruskin's death in January 1900, Proust wrote to Marie Nordlinger of his sadness and yet of his consolation, realizing "how paltry a thing death is when I see how vigorously this dead man still lives, how I admire him." Although a time would come when he was no longer obsessed with Ruskin, the imprint of Ruskin's style and language — and through it the resonance of the King James Bible — was gloriously ineradicable. Of Proust's work

John Ruskin (1819-1900), British writer, Self-Portrait in Blue Neckcloth. *Watercolor.*

mieux venu, le plus frappant et le plus célèbre[1], et pour mieux dire, jusqu'à ce jour, le seul, c'est le Ruskin qui n'a connu toute sa vie qu'une religion : celle de la Beauté.

Que l'adoration de la Beauté ait été, en effet, l'acte perpétuel de la vie de Ruskin, cela peut être vrai à la lettre ; mais j'estime que le but de cette vie, son intention profonde, secrète et constante était autre, et si je le dis, ce n'est pas pour m'écarter des vues de M. de la Sizeranne, mais pour empêcher qu'elles ne soient rabaissées dans l'esprit des lecteurs par une interprétation fausse, mais naturelle et comme inévitable.

Non seulement la principale religion de Ruskin fut la Religion tout court (et je reviendrai sur ce point tout à l'heure, car il domine et caractérise son esthétique), mais, pour nous en tenir en ce moment à la « Religion de la Beauté », il faudrait avertir notre temps qu'il ne peut prononcer ces mots, s'il veut faire une allusion juste à Ruskin, qu'en redressant le sens que son dilettantisme esthétique est trop porté à leur donner. Pour notre âge, en effet, de dilettantes et d'esthètes, un adorateur de la Beauté, c'est un homme qui, ne pratiquant pas d'autre culte et ne reconnaissant pas d'autre dieu, passerait sa vie dans la jouissance que donne la contemplation voluptueuse des œuvres d'art.

Or, pour des raisons dont la recherche toute métaphysique dépasserait une simple étude d'art, la Beauté ne peut être aimée d'une manière féconde si on l'aime seulement pour les plaisirs qu'elle donne. Et, de même que la recherche du bonheur pour lui-même n'atteint que l'ennui, et qu'il faut pour le trouver chercher autre chose que lui, de même le plaisir esthétique nous est donné par surcroît si nous aimons la Beauté pour elle-même, comme quelque chose de réel existant en dehors de nous et infiniment plus important que la joie qu'elle nous donne. Et, très loin d'avoir été un dilettante ou un esthète, Ruskin fut précisément le contraire, un de ces hommes à la Carlyle, averti par leur génie de la vanité de tout plaisir et, en même temps, de la présence auprès d'eux d'une réalité éternelle, intuitivement perçue par l'inspiration. Le talent leur est donné comme un pouvoir de fixer cette réalité à la toute-puissance et à l'éternité de laquelle ils consacrent, pour lui donner quelque valeur, avec enthousiasme et comme obéissant à un commandement de la conscience, leur vie éphémère. De tels hommes, attentifs et anxieux devant l'univers à déchiffrer, sont avertis des parties de la réalité

1. Le Ruskin de M. de la Sizeranne.

Above: *Contract with Mercure de France, for translation of Ruskin's La Bible d'Amiens, February 26, 1904.*

Left: *Article by Proust, from the Gazette des Beaux-Arts, with manuscript corrections, about "Ruskin, who knew his whole life long only one religion: Beauty."*

with Marie Nordlinger on the translation, the philosopher Henri Bergson found it so alive and so original "that one would never suspect the work of being a translation."

Among other things Ruskinian, Proust was enthusiastic about the way in which Ruskin the master and a band of young enthusiasts would visit monuments together, and indeed on Good Friday, April 10, 1903, he too set out for a visit to the churches of Laon, Coucy, Senlis, Soissons, and some others. Accompanying him were Georges de Lauris, Robert de Billy, and the brothers Bibesco — Antoine and his homosexual brother Emmanuel, who was to hang himself in despair over his situation, finding it unworthy of the son of a great family. Proust was for some years close to Antoine, desiring to be closer and believing in their "oneness," but given the latter's interest in womanizing, they eventually became only friends, dissolving the odd pact in which each would tell the other all his secrets, eschewing all jealousy and envy. Proust was to accuse Antoine of not telling him a sufficient number of secrets to make "the tomb" or the secrecy interesting, and Antoine was pained by Proust's returning to him a fur overcoat he had proffered to keep the eternally chilly writer warm. The latter's excuse was his unwillingness to hurt his brother Robert, who had similarly offered him one. In a letter of March 1904, he accuses the "wicked fairy" of Antoine's self-destructive character of forcing all his previous traits to become just the vestiges of their former selves, but declares himself nonetheless joyous to see in his physical person "the unconscious memory of the marvelous qualities you once had." The role of memory, ever more important in Proustian perception, shows itself everywhere, even in what might seem its most trivial occurrences.

To thank Marie Nordlinger for her help in translating Ruskin (they would pore over the work sometimes in St. Mark's or across from it, at Florian's), Proust gave her Montesquiou's own copy of Whistler's *Gentle Art of Making Enemies.* The gift was particularly ironic, in view of Whistler's own mockery of Ruskin, and his transcription of the proceedings of his lawsuit against Ruskin, who had accused him of being a coxcomb and "throwing a pot of paint in the public's eye" with his

James Abbott McNeill Whistler, Nocturne in Blue and Silver: Chelsea, 1871.

high-priced *Nocturne in Blue and Silver*. How long, had the judge asked, did it take you to paint this picture? A day, responded Whistler . . . and the knowledge of a lifetime.

When Proust had removed from his bedroom every vestige of the purely aesthetic, including his photograph of the Amiens Cathedral, Whistler's Carlyle remained. About this, he had written Marie Nordlinger when she was in America and had made friends with the millionaire Charles Freer, whose collection of Whistlers was the finest in the world and who had commissioned Whistler's *Peacock Room*. "Tell your friend," he wrote, "that my room contains in its intentional nudity only a single reproduction of a work of art — Whistler's Carlyle, whose cloak is as serpentine in its folds as the gown of Whistler's Mother." On June 15, 1905, staying up all day to do so, he visited the Whistler exhibition at the École des Beaux-Arts, and saw there landscapes of "Venice in turquoise, Holland in topaz, Brittany in opal" —Whistler's *La Plage d'Opale* (The Opal Beach), to which Legrandin's mention of "the Opal Bay near Balbec" alludes.

Proust had met Whistler at the home of Mallarmé's mistress, Méry Laurent, where he had "appropriated his elegant gray gloves, which I've lost since." Mallarmé had sent Méry some bit of botan-ical wisdom, saying it would give her a chance to show off for Proust — whom he never met. The artistic appropriation of the gloves casts an amusing reflec-tion on Proust's own conception of morality, his loyalties divided between Whistler's point of view about art being separate from morality and the view of Ruskin. ("Whistler is right . . . and yet Ruskin too, utters a truth, though on a different level, when he says

Stéphane Mallarmé and Méry Laurent.

that all great art is a form of morality.") Proust's prefatory essay ("Sur la lecture") to his translation of Ruskin, *Sésame et les lys*, stresses the recollection of past memories in art, whereas Ruskin conceived of it as a conversation with those wiser and more interesting than ourselves.

Proust follows impassioned in Ruskin's footsteps, making his pilgrimage to the cathedral at Amiens to see the *Gilded Angel*, stopping at just the *pâtisserie* Ruskin recommends in *The Bible of Amiens*, delighted when Marie finds just the tiny statue Ruskin mentions. His own devotion to details others might overlook had a good part of its training in his devotion to the Master. His 1908 notebook, providing rich material for detail-seekers, lists all sorts of things he cared about: from smells to soap, from names of places and people to perfumes. He, like Ruskin, was one of the greatest observers ever: tombstones and stained-glass windows, the sky and the grass. Little seems to escape their notice, from beginning to end, their obsessive writing leaving traces everywhere of their all-inclusive staring. Reynaldo Hahn's composition in 1900, after Ruskin's disappearance — *The Muses Mourning the Death of Ruskin* — is dedicated to Proust. And Proust's defense of French cathedrals in a time of rabid anti-clericalism was given its original energy by Ruskin's own love of them.

If Proust was eventually to criticize Ruskin's idolatry of the graven image over the truth it represented, and to separate his own opinions from those he had so long admired without qualification, Ruskin was an essential source of his vision and style, throughout the exhausting labor. His essay "On Reading" marks his return to, and the beginnings of, his great novel, and its fifty pages are substituted for Ruskin's own preface. After translating Ruskin, he said, he wanted to "try to translate my own soul, if it doesn't die in the meantime." Perhaps the major element he was to retain from Ruskin was the conviction that the task of writing is "infinitely more important than life"and so is the path to salvation, of the kind to which his *Search* is dedicated, as was Ruskin's entire work.

That notebook of 1908, in which he wrote once about creating worlds, led him to more notebooks, written between 1908 and 1909, which were to become, after his death, the pages of *Against Sainte-Beuve*. This same variety of school notebook, easily available and on such modest quality paper, is the direct opposite of the deluxe edition of *Pleasures and Days* he had wanted earlier to prepare for an exclusive readership. The latter was dedicated to the elegant Willie Heath, whom he met in 1892 and who died in the fall of the same year. The dedication read: "We had the dream, almost a project, of living more and more with each other, in a circle of men and women magnanimous and chosen, far enough away from stupidity, vice and meanness, to find ourselves sheltered from their vulgar arrows." But, as Ruskin felt, in his later work and at his best, that he was writing for a universal audience — the working class — so did Proust. Since he was paying the expenses of the publication of his novel, to give himself the freedom he must have known he would require for the more than massive revisions, he wanted also to be able to set the price. He was adamant about not wanting his thoughts to be reserved "for people who spend ten francs on a book and are generally stupider than those who buy them for three." In fact, his ideal readers, as he says towards the end of his life, are the true friends that will read it in the metro, "oblivious to those sitting next to them and ride past their stops." A note for *Against*

Willie Heath.

Sainte-Beuve invokes the young man living within the grown writer:

> "*Who dies instantly in the particular, and begins immediately to float and live in the general . . . But while he lives, his life is only ecstasy and felicity. He alone should write my books: The young man who . . . plays among my ruins lives on air; the pleasure he draws from the sight of the idea he has discovered is all the food he needs; he creates the idea and is created by it; he dies, but an idea survives him — like those seeds which suspend the process of germination in too dry an atmosphere and are lifeless; but a little moisture and warmth is enough to bring them back to life.*"

The only people superior to their writing, he says, are those "whose books are not really Books."

The essential thing is to pass on whatever idea one cares about, from one form, one person, one generation to another. Proust's fervid attachment to Thomas Hardy went far past the idea of seeking the traits of one incarnation of a family characteristic to the next, as in Hardy's *The Well-Beloved* —his tale of a man loving, at different times in his life, a girl, her daughter, and her daughter's daughter — although there are several traces of that sharing of traits in his depiction of the Guermantes family and in his interrogation of his friends about other similar cases. Proust, already acquainted with Hardy's *Jude the Obscure* and *A Pair of Blue Eyes*, was to realize above all the importance of "the stone-mason's geometry of Hardy's novels." For the similar nature of all the works of a great artist and the presence of a singular theme in each — like the little musical phrase the Narrator of the *Search* hears and is obsessed by, from a composition of the musician called Vinteuil (a combination of César Franck, Gabriel Fauré, and others), and the parallel possibility of recurrence of figures and emotions, translating each other, or passing down through the generations — takes on an ever-increasing significance. As the essential idea passes from one form to another, the salvation of the artist — and everyone else — constructs itself.

Looking and Listening

Proust's passion for paintings is well known. To him, the most wonderful painting in the world was Vermeer's *View of Delft*, which he first saw on October 18, 1902, in the Mauritshuis Royal Art Gallery in The Hague. Unforgettably, in front of that painting the writer Bergotte — a composite of Ruskin, other writers, and himself — measures his own creation and collapses. When asked, in a questionnaire sent by Halévy to many well-known authors, which paintings from the Louvre should be

Below: Jan Vermeer (1632-1675), View of Delft, ca. 1658.

Above left: *Jean-Baptiste Simeon Chardin (1699-1779),* Self-Portait at His Easel, *1776.*

Above right: *Jean-Baptiste Simeon Chardin (1699-1779),* The Buffet, *1728.*

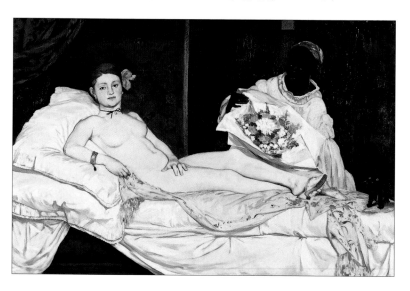

Above: Jean Antoine Watteau (1684-1721). The Embarkation for Cythera, 1717.

Left: Édouard Manet (1832-1883), Olympia, 1863.

exhibited first of all, he replied that he would have chosen Chardin with his self-portrait, his portrait of his wife, and a still life, Millet's *Springtime*, Manet's *Olympia*; a Renoir, Corot's *Dante's Boat*, or his *Chartres Cathedral*, and Watteau's *Embarkation for Cythera*. But the painter with the most impact on his novel, and perhaps his imagination, was surely Carpaccio.

It is a cloak by Mariano de Fortuny that he will place on the shoulders of the Carpaccio in *The Fugitive*, describing to Madame Straus that Carpaccio's *Patriarch of Grado Exorcising a Demoniac*: "There is quite a flowering of bellmouthed chimneys, as beautiful as a shower of tulips, and I would not be surprised if it had helped to inspire some of Whistler's little Venice pictures." He refuses her offer to lend him her Fortuny coat, preferring to think only about the painting. His obsessions such as this one lead implicitly to the great text, for as he says to her: "The result will be a line here and there, but even to say one word about something, and sometimes even not to mention it at all, I need to get reproductions of Carpaccio."

Above: *Vittore Carpaccio (1455-1525),* The Meeting of the Betrothed Couple and the Departure of the Pilgrims, *from the* Legend of Saint Ursula, *1495.*

Left: *Claude Monet (1840-1926),* Cathedral of Rouen, Portal and Saint-Romain Tower, Full Sunlight, Harmony in Blue and Gold, *1894.*

Right: *Décor for Claude Debussy's* Pelléas et Mélisande, *by L. Jusseaume. First set: The Forest, the prelude for the first act, at the Opéra-comique de Paris, 1902.*

On May 9, 1910, he breaks with his sleeping habits in the same way he had for exhibitions of Vermeer and Whistler. He goes to the Durand-Ruel Gallery to see Monet's "forty-eight sonnets" of water lilies, and to the Bernheim-Jeune Gallery to see twenty-eight paintings of Venice. He never went to Giverny to see the painter, but the Strauses had several Monets, and his viewing of the work was clearly what mattered to him. The painter's way of handling his various series must have been much in his mind in his own writing, perhaps especially Monet's repeated views of the Rouen cathedral, even as Proust alleges for himself a more modest approach, constructing his book — imagining himself alongside Françoise — "I dare not say ambitiously like a cathedral, but quite simply like a dress."

And on April 21, 1921, Vermeer's *View of Delft* returned to Paris, so that Proust was able to see it once more. He had written the passage about Bergotte succumbing in front of this "most beautiful painting in the world" with its "little patch of yellow wall" twenty years before, when he had first seen it in Holland. Similarly, his musical obsessions are connected with his own work in implicit fashion, with its interwoven narratives and its way of announcing and following the lines. If he preferred the subtlety and melancholy of Debussy's *Pelléas et Mélisande* to Wagner's *Die Meistersinger*, of

Echo

Notre ami Marcel Proust dont les lecteurs du Figaro connaissent les pastiches a une immense admiration pour le Pelléas et Mélisande de Debussy. L'autre jour il sortait d'une réunion avec un ami qui ne pouvait pas trouver son chapeau. Marcel Proust imagina le duo suivant. Que le lecteur mette sous les questions la déclamation pressante, rapide, sous les réponses la gravité mélancolique, la mystérieuse cantilène de Debussy et il sentira le juste... extrême de la petite pastiche non pas de la pièce de Maeterlinck, mais du livret de Debussy (il y a une nuance)

Markel :
« Vous avez un tort de laisser le chapeau ! Vous ne le retrouverez jamais !
Pelléas :
« Pourquoi ne le retrouverais-je pas ? »

M.
« On ne retrouve jamais rien . . . . . ici . . .
Il est perdu pour toujours »
P.
« En nous en allant nous en prendrons un,
— qui lui ressemble ! »
M. « Il n'y a pas qui lui ressemble ! »
P. « Comment était-il donc ? »
M. très ~~lentement~~ de ce ...
« C'était un pauvre petit chapeau
Comme en porte tout le monde !
Personne n'aurait pu dire de chez qui il venait . . . Il avait l'air de venir du bout du monde . .
Maintenant il ne faut plus le chercher car nous ne le retrouverions pas.
P. « Il me semble que ma tête commence à avoir froid pour toujours. Il fait un

Echo

grand froid dehors. C'est l'hiver !
Si encore le soleil n'était pas couché
Pourquoi avait-on laissé la fenêtre ou-
verte. Il faisait dehors une atmosphère
lourde et empoisonnée, et j'ai ~~longue~~ (cru que)
j'allais me trouver mal. Et maintenant
tout l'air de toute la Terre !
M.
Vous avez, Pelléas, le visage grave et
plein de larmes que ceux qui ne sont
enrhumés pour longtemps ! Allons-
nous en. Nous ne le retrouverons pas.
Quelqu'un qui n'est pas d'ici l'aura
emporté et Dieu sait où l'a en ce mo-
Il est trop tard. Tous les autres chapeaux sont
partis. Nous ne pourrons plus prendre un autre.
C'est une chose terrible, Pelléas. Mais ce n'est pas
votre faute.
Quelle est la fin ?

Pastiche of Pelléas: Instead of a lost ring, as in the opera, a hat is lost. "Let the reader suppose under the questions the hurried, urgent speech, under the answers the melancholy gravity, the mysterious cantilène of Debussy and he will feel the fittingness of the little pastiche, not of Maeterlinck's play but Debussy's libretto (nuance.)"

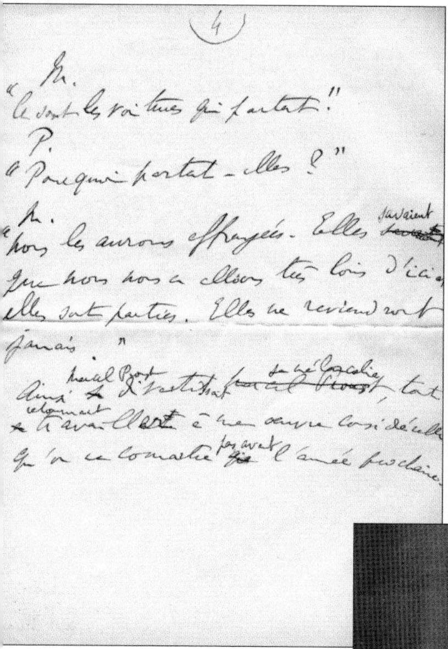
(4)

M.
« Ce sont les voitures qui partent ! »
P.
« Pourquoi partent-elles ? »
M.
« Nous les aurons effrayées. Elles savaient que nous nous en allions très loin d'ici, elles sont parties. Elles ne reviendront jamais. »

Ainsi [illegible] Marcel Proust [illegible], tout [illegible] à travaillé à une œuvre considérable qu'on ne connaîtra pas avant l'année prochaine.

Below: *Sarah Bernhardt in the role of Pelléas in* Pelléas et Mélisande *by Maurice Maeterlinck, London, 1907.*

which only one act sufficed to let him counter Reynaldo's profession of admiration for the piece, it was the words as well as the melody that delighted him. He was so impassioned about the opera, and the words by Maurice Maeterlinck — that great writer of allegories about bees and ants — that each evening it was staged, he would request the Théâtrophone operator to let him listen to the performance, canceling anything else he had planned. That miraculous instrument, which broadcast from eight Paris theaters the sound through telephone lines to cafés and private subscribers, from 1881 for several years, was essential to Proust's world. As for

AUDITIONS THÉATRALES A DOMICILE
23, rue Louis-le-Grand, 23
PARIS

Ad for the "Théâtrophone," a system of microphones on stage linked to telephone lines, invented by Clément Ader, and first tried out at the Opéra and the l'Opéra-Comique in 1881. It permitted the audition of theatrical performances at home.

Pélleas, there is not, he said to his friends, in the whole opera, "one word that does not come back to me." He would sing it over to

Debussy, Pelléas et Mélisande, Act III, Scene I.

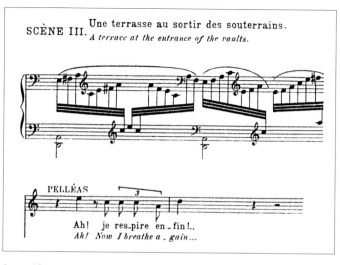

himself repeatedly, taking the part of Pélleas, whose emergence into the daylight he preferred above all others — which would make sense for an asthmatic sufferer. "Ah, I breathe at last," he would say with Pélleas, and the words are reminiscent of the passage in the first part of the *Search*, describing the Narrator's grandmother (clearly a stand-in for his mother and her attributes) with her love of things natural, as she turns her face up to the rain. At other times he would send a pastiche to Reynaldo, ascribing to him the part of Pélleas, calling himself Markel, a combination of Marcel and Arkel, the father of Golaud. "There are some phrases truly impregnated with the freshness of the sea and the smell of roses carried by the breeze," he wrote to Antoine Bibesco. He had had, he said, "the misfortune of hearing Pélleas on the Théâtrophone and falling in love with it." Sadly, he found Debussy's *The Martyrdom of Saint Sebastian* "very boring," although it was interpreted by Ida Rubinstein, whom he so admired in *Schéhérazade*.

Among the principal hinges between Proust's outside and inside worlds were the occasions on which he saw a particular exhibition or heard a particular concert. Meeting Gabriel Fauré, one of his favorite composers of all time, particularly for his Sonata for Violin and Piano

très crâne et avec élégance (non troppo legato)

Les donneurs ___ de sé_ré _ na _ _ des

p

en marquant légèrement la basse

Reynaldo Hahn, music set to a poem by Paul Verlaine.

no. 1 in D Minor, at a concert of his chamber music, he asked him for an introduction to the Poulet Quartet, whose members Gaston Poulet, Louis Ruyssen, Victor Gentil, and Amable Massis he paid to play for him Beethoven's Opus 130, Quartet in B flat major and César Franck's quartet. In the candlelit room, Proust reposed on a divan of green velvet, with his eyes closed. When they had finished, at two in the morning, he asked them to play it all again. His intensity of listening imbued his work; we recognize in the text, as in the music, the same haunting strains over and over. He was eager to attend Georges Enesco's rendering of the violin part and Paul Goldschmidt's of the piano part in César Franck's 1886 *Sonata in A major for Piano and Violin.* Together with Franck's Quartet in D Major and his Piano Quintet in F Minor (which announced the Sonata of seven years later), Saint-Saëns's Sonata in D Minor, Fauré's *Ballade*, and Debussy's *La Mer*, these led directly to Vinteuil's Sonata and other compositions. In the draft of the Vinteuil recital at the casino in Balbec, Proust wrote a memo to himself: "Franck's Quintet (call it

IV

Allegretto poco mosso

dolce cantabile

Allegretto poco mosso

dolce cantabile

sempre legato

César Franck: Sonata in A Major for Piano and Violin.

something else)." He would go to hear Beethoven quartets whenever he could. Meditating about one such occasion, attending a performance of the *Twelfth Quartet*, Proust wrote to a friend: "For several years Beethoven's late quartets and Franck's music have been my primary spiritual nourishment."

Proust's overwhelming love of all these composers converges in his well-known passages on the composer Vinteuil, whose little phrase, affecting and recurring in the Narrator's consciousness as an emotive leitmotif reflects the sources just mentioned. To this group, Wagner should be added, as one of Proust's musical passions, in particular because of the prelude to the first act of *Lohengrin* and the "Good Friday Spell" from *Parsifal*. This was the moment of a general fever for Wagner, with pilgrimages made to Bayreuth by the Countess Greffulhe and by Montesquiou, Reynaldo Hahn, and Jacques-Émile Blanche. Albert Lavignac's

Fran Cocteau

✗   1954

"practical guidebook for the Frenchman in Bayreuth," went into five editions. "The more legendary Wagner is, the more human I find him, and in him the most magnificent artifice of the imagination strikes me only as the compelling symbolic expression of moral truths."

Proust was a great watcher, and his affection for the vivid spectacle of society was for a time easily congruent with that for the spectacle of culture. In 1906, there had been a great exhibition of Russian art in the Grand Palais for the Salon d'Automne, with the backing of the intimates of the Greffulhes in banking and diplomatic circles. Sergei Diaghilev, who had visited the painter and patron Jacques-Émile Blanche at Dieppe in 1893 and was welcome in French artistic circles, was named the Commissaire Générale de l'Exposition. In his welcoming speech, he made a grand claim: "We are witnesses of the greatest moment of summing-up in history, in the name of a new and unknown culture, which will be created by us, and which will also sweep us away." As a background for the exhibition, the designer Léon Bakst created one of his exotic sets. Diaghilev was offered the Legion d'Honneur after this, and, with his usual generosity, suggested that it be presented to Bakst and Benois, the designers. Speaking of Diaghilev's remarkable personality, Nijinsky claimed his influence as the greatest anyone had had on him. "He was a genius, a great

Nijinsky, Russian dancer, as the Golden Slave in Diaghilev's Schéhérézade.

organizer, pioneer and discoverer of talents, with the soul of an artist and manners of a nobleman." Continuing his relation to Paris, in 1908 Diaghilev brought there the opera *Boris Godunov*, and attending a performance of it, the lovely Misia Sert Edwards was fascinated to the extent of declaring: "I left the theatre stirred to the point of realising that something had changed in my life." Thereafter she was the intimate friend and supporter of Diaghilev, by whose side she usually attended the theater. Diaghilev's whole conception of the ballet was that of Wagner's *Gesamtkunstwerk*, the total art work.

Diaghilev brought the Ballets Russes to Paris in 1909, for a brief visit, and then again in 1910. Proust attended the opening night at the Opera on June 4, with the celebrated composer, his faithful friend, Reynaldo Hahn, and the art critic Jean-Louis Vaudoyer, to see the dancers Nijinsky and Ida Rubinstein in *Schéhérazade*. The stage was as colorful as the dancing, bedecked with an orange carpet, a green tent, and blue doors, a perfect set for Rubinstein's cavorting as the Sultan's favorite wife, and Nijinsky's immensely popular death throes. "I never saw anything so beautiful," said Proust. He particularly liked the personality of Bakst, caring far less for the person of Nijinsky. For the latter's dancing, nothing seemed too strong. As one critic says of his performance as the Slave in *Schehérézade*: "This strange, curious, head-wagging, simian crea-ture, scarcely human, wriggled through the play, leaving a long streak of lust and terror in his wake," and one of society's minor poets but major figures, Anna de Noailles, said of his performance in *Cléopatre*, "The angel, the genius, the triumpher of the spectacle, the divine dancer Nijinsky . . . He took hold of our hearts." Indeed, Anna de Noailles was a very noisy enthusiast. André Gide describes, in his journal for July 1, 1910, how Henri de Régnier called upon him upon such an occasion at one rehearsal: "M. Gide," exclaimed M. de Régnier, "come and help us calm Mme de Noailles." She was talking at such a volume and with such gestures that the attention of half the audience was focused upon her.

In any case, the world of Proust or the "Tout-Proust," as it was called, comprised many society persons, patrons of the Diaghilev

Left: Édouard Manet (1832-1883), The Asparagus, 1880. Near the beginning of the novel, Françoise serves asparagus frequently, because their smell sickens the pregnant kitchen maid, whom the narrator always compares to Giotto's fresco, La Charité.

Below: Giotto di Bondone (1266-1336), La Charité, 1302-1305.

circle, among them the Princesse Edmond de Polignac (the American heiress, Winaretta Singer or "Tante Winnie"), as well as Montesquiou, the painter Jacques-Émile Blanche, Proust's close friend and lover, the musician/composer Reynaldo Hahn, and the art collector and enormously learned director of the *Gazette des Beaux-Arts*, Charles Ephrussi (one of the inspirations for Swann, and the patron who had overpaid Manet for a still life of asparagus, to whom the painter then famously sent one more spear). When Diaghilev needed for his programs Reynaldo Hahn,

a musical conservative with little time for the innovators, who was even hostile to Wagner, he had only to stage the latter's work *Le Dieu bleu* — a fair exchange for both parties.

Le Spectre de la Rose had as its set a white and blue room, where the windows gave onto a nocturnal garden. The ballerina Tamara Karsavina wore a white dress with a wide flounce, her white cape tied under her chin, and Nijinsky wore an androgynous costume of pink and lilac tights, along with a cap of the same petals. About his dancing, the critic Paul Magriel enthused: "One can only compare him with himself. . . . His dancing has the unbroken quality of music, the balance of great painting, the meaning of fine literature . . . The delicacy with which he cantilevers the weight actually displaced keeps the firmness from being rigidity . . . all of it relates to a clear center which is not altered." When he was not dancing, his body seemed short and ineffective. But his personal magnetism when staged was enormous: when he was in London, the entire Bloomsbury group seems to have fallen in love with him. Maynard Keynes would come down from Cambridge to take a look at Nijinsky's legs; Lytton Strachey would wear a particular purple costume, hoping to meet Nijinsky, and sent "magnissime" flowers over to Drury Lane. A few would dress as Nijinksy and Karsavina at their parties, and would even enact their ballets; at Ottoline Morrel's Thursday parties, they would dress Oriental Style, again influenced by the Ballets Russes. Duncan Grant was intrigued by Nijinsky, and the attraction was mutual: "I saw Nijinsky looking him all over," said Ottoline. But conversation was difficult, if not impossible, given any language other than that of the eyes. Lytton Strachey overheard Ottoline in desperate effusions of attempted communication: "'Quand vous dansez, vous n'êtes pas un homme — vous êtes une idée. C'est ça, n'est-ce pas, qui est l'Art?, . . .? Vous avez lu Platon, sans doute?'—The reply was a grunt." Clearly, she had read her Mallarmé, in his essays on "Ballets," and on the American dancer Loie Fuller, in which he says the ballerina is not a woman but a sign, an idea. Perhaps Nijinsky had not read the same

Above left: Nijinsky's costume of pink and
lilac tights for Le Spectre de la Rose.
The ballet premiered on May 13, 1912.

Above right: Tamara Karsavina's costume
sketch.

Right: Valentine Hugo, poster for Nijinsky,
dancing in Le Spectre de la Rose.

things . . . In May 1914, Loie Fuller performed at the Théâtre de Châtelet in Paris, to general acclaim. It was precisely not her body that mattered (if Nijinsky was short, Fuller was rather plump), but her illusion-creation, again like that of Nijinsky.

There is and has been for some years, including those in which Proust lived, a cult of Nijinsky, which his naïveté, childlike behavior, and his later schizophrenia did nothing to quell. Yet the musicians' point of view about him was not always the expected one. Stravinsky wrote: "Of all the choreographers I have ever collaborated with N. was the least musical; he, however, had a singular talent which outweighed all that. To call him a dancer would only be half of the truth, because to an even greater degree he was a dramatic actor."

In her chapter on "The Vanguard Poetic of Vaslav Nijinksy," Lynn Garafola sketches Nijinsky's career with his four Ballets Russes – for one thing, until *Schéhérazade*, the ballerina had always taken precedence; now it was the turn of the male dancer. Nijinsky's ballets after that were *L'Après-midi d'un Faune* (1912), *Jeux* (1913), *Le Sacre du Printemps* (1913), and *Till Eulenspiegel*. (1916). Nijinsky conceived of *Jeux* as a game of tennis interrupted by an airplane overhead – neoclassicism and futurism together – we might remember a few photographs of the young Marcel with friends and a tennis racket, and, more distressingly, his anguish

Program cover by Léon Bakst (1866-1924) of Nijinsky dancing in La Péri, *1911.*

over Agostinelli's plane crash. Nijinsky wrote in his diary of his attraction to sports: "The close study I have made of polo, golf, and tennis, has convinced me that these sports are not only a healthy form of relaxation but that they are equally creators of plastic beauty." The story of *Jeux* is the game of three young men making love to each other, which can be interpreted as so many "mirror images of the protagonist's compound sexual identity," unlike the erotic fantasies of the Faun. When Nijinsky plays the Golden Slave, in *Schéhérazade*, or *Le Spectre de la Rose*, he is clearly acting the part as a homosexual. But his marriage to Romola de Pulszky in 1913, shows him as a covert heterosexual, all the more complicated a role, and all the more fascinating for present-day readers and balletomanes. For us, he figures as the idiot savant, holy fool, and as the "clone of God" he repeatedly calls himself in his diaries.

Léon Bakst (1866-1924), Set design for the ballet Schéhérazade, *by Rimsky-Korsakoff. Decoration for the Harem. Watercolor, 1916.*

Nijinsky only split with Diaghilev at the time of his marriage: then he was forced to leave the Ballets Russes, through Diaghilev's jealousy. Diaghilev then found, as choreographer, Léonide Massine, plucked straight from the Bolshoi corps de ballet. The Ballets Russes continued, of course, with Stravinsky's *Rite of Spring* and the collaborative work in 1917 of three geniuses in *Parade*: Cocteau, Picasso, and Satie. But at this point, Cocteau broke with Diaghilev, when the latter eliminated all the sounds he had wanted in *Parade*: typewriters, the tapping out of Morse code, sirens, and the hoots of an express train

Cocteau's celebrated posters for the Ballets Russes included advertisements for Nijinsky in Fokine's 1910 ballet *Schéhérazade*, inspired by Rimsky-Korsakov's music – such an inspiration to him that he founded a journal with that name, to which Reynaldo Hahn and others were contributors. He made a poster also of Nijinsky and Karsavina in *Le Spectre de la Rose*, in 1911. Bakst's famous costumes freed back and midriff for dancing: "He dressed his women in tunics and harem pants, soft flowing garments that released the torso from the constricting bodice of the tutu . . . His harem pants followed the curve of the buttocks as did the panels of tunics tacked together high at the thigh." This natural unfettered body gave an "impression of nakedness and naturalness." Isadora Duncan, who had danced in bare feet in St. Petersburg in 1904, 1907, and 1909, at

Right: Vaslav Nijinsky, in the ballet Orientales, *dancing in the garden of the painter Jacques-Émile Blanche, June 19, 1910.*

el Duncan
grant son ami Lisieux

the time of Fokine's initial undertakings, had a clear influence on Bakst's Grecian-inspired garments of a "sublime simplicity."

Her influence on the Ballets Russes cannot be overestimated, in part for her communicated enthusiasm for the classic world. Bakst and Diaghilev had gone to Greece in 1907, and were especially impressed with Minoan Greece, Mycenae, Knossos, and early Greek sculpture. The statuesque and undancerly slow motion of the *L'Après-midi d'un faune*, with the words of Mallarmé and the music of Debussy, expresses a kind of "inner rhythm." The eight-minute dance showed, in its controversial final scene of masturbation, as nothing else could, Nijinsky's own "deep-rooted ambivalence toward men and women alike." The sculptor Auguste Rodin said of this work: "I hope that such a masterpiece as *L'Après-midi d'un faune* will be duly understood and appreciated and that it will become a model of genuine beauty for all men of art without exception."

Diaghilev's ballets were international in scope and setting, with infusions of the oriental and the exotic, their inspirations drawn from the Bible and Islam, from Africa, Iran, India, Japan, and China. The staged visual opulence attracted the same in the spectators. Paul Morand comments on "The boldness of the audience's dress, its immodesties, extravagant coiffures, depilated bodies, cosmetics." Among the enthusiasts in the audience, was the melodramatic and outlandish Montesquiou, noticeable not only for his more than singular pose but for his unstoppable and ornamented discourse, for his arrogance beyond belief. Captivated by the boyish figure of Ida Rubinstein, one of the so-called "Jewesses of art" in Paris in this epoch — who was later the perfect Saint Sebastian in Debussy's opera about his martyrdom (so disliked by Proust) — Montesquiou attended every single performance, which was good for publicity, given his remarkable way of dressing and posturing.

Proust also became an assiduous attendee of the Ballets Russes in the summers of the next years, in his fur coat, with his black-rimmed eyes and pale face (once described as Belgian endives left too long in a cellar) striking in any audience. In the master's box, Diaghilev would sit, looking at his dancers through his mother-of-pearl lorgnette, with the beautiful Misia Edwards beside him, a tall feather in her hair. If Diaghilev the genius was unmistakable in his conceptions and his all-inclusive passions, his person was no less so. Jean Cocteau describes him: "His dancers called him Chinchilla because of an isolated white lock in his very dark dyed hair. He wore a tightly fitting fur coat and an opossum collar and at times he buttoned it up with safety pins. His face was a bull dog's, his smile a very young crocodile's, one tooth on the edge. To grind this tooth was for him a sign of pleasure, or fear, or anger. . . . And his wet eye looking downward had the curve of a Portuguese oyster." Misia, once married to Thadée Natanson, editor of the symbolist journal *La Revue Blanche* and a close friend of many symbolists, including the poet Stéphane Mallarmé and the painter Édouard Vuillard, was now the wife of the stage designer José Maria Sert.

Proust had agonized with her during the long dinners in Cabourg's Grand Hôtel in 1907. The seaside town was the major source for the novel's Balbec, along with the Breton town Beg-Meil, where Proust had written the first part of *Jean Santeuil*, which he described as nothing more than an "apple-orchard sloping down to a sleepy bay."[4] In the odd sleeping arrangements on the floor above the dining room, Edwards was accompanied not just by his wife, but by his mistress the actress Geneviève Lantelme, presumably at least partially lesbian, whose former husband, Dr. Charcot, was nearby, as was Natanson. Trying to imitate Lantelme's hair style and clothes, Misia inspired the situation in which Gilberte imitates Rachel, in hopes of pleasing Saint-Loup. Lantelme drowned, in peculiar circumstances, off the Edwards' yacht, in 1911, and someone is said to have remarked of his next mistress that he certainly hoped she could swim.

Post-ballet, at Larue's, the restaurant at the corner of the rue Royale and the Madeleine, Proust would sit with Diaghilev and Nijinsky, having a hot chocolate instead of the immense steaks they were consuming, write his flowery letters, excusing this and that, and beg for some detail of dress or custom from someone who would know just the precise detail. Everything had to be exact.

Jean Cocteau, a friend of Diaghilev, who had commissioned him to compose a scenario for Hahn's *Le Dieu bleu*, was an elegant thin man about town and of the theater, and the center of a certain gay culture. His troubled, ironic, and mannered plays and prose works were a barometer of the time. Like Proust's beloved Fénelon, like Saint-Loup in the novel, Cocteau once leapt upon the table and running along the benches, shouting "It's Marcel!"

The pilgrim in Reynaldo Hahn's Le Dieu bleu, *after Léon Bakst's watercolor, 1912.*

rushed to drape his satin and mink cloak over the shivering shoulders of Proust, already enclosed in his fur coat.

> *To cover my shoulders with satin-lined mink*
> *Without spilling one drop from his huge eyes' black ink*
> *Like a sylph to the ceiling, or on snow a thin ski,*
> *Jean leaped on a table and dropped by Nijinsk.*

Cocteau said of Proust, whom he much admired, when the latter would reproach him for faults in friendship he was unaware of having committed, that he must have, because, in the case of Proust always, "he was right."[5]

At Proust's other favorite restaurant, the Ritz, he would attend and give dinner after dinner, with the Princess Soutzo, the Countess Étienne de Beaumont, his good friend Walter Berry, and his favorite priest, the endlessly good-tempered and witty Abbé Mugnier, the Vicar of St. Clothilde, who felt in himself a particular mission for ministering to the needs of the ladies of the night: "I have to take care of mes poules," he would say. He was noted for having converted, in 1892, the writer Joris-Karl Huysmans, author of the

Above: *Joris-Karl Huysmans (1848-1907), French writer, in 1905.*

Left: *Princess Soutzo.*

Right: *The Dining room of the Hotel Ritz, the place Vendôme, Paris, in 1939.*

far-out symbolist novel *À rebours* (Against the Grain), whose super-bizarre hero Des Esseintes is closely based on Montesquiou, who indeed lined his pet tortoise's tummy with jewels and made other such endearing gestures.

At the Ritz, Proust would have his special needs answered, with a table set up for him at any of the odd hours he chose. He could be found at four in the morning, at a special table under the stairs, with the watchful and ever-useful headwaiter, Olivier Dabescat, providing a temperature of 86, and a fire before which Proust would sit bundled up, of course, in his overcoat over his evening dress. He and Dabescat would linger over their gossip about the frequenters of the Ritz, and sometimes Dabescat would come to Proust's flat to continue the discussion, between midnight when he was through with his service and 3 or 4 A.M. One of the more celebrated anecdotes of Proust's extravagance and generosity, depending upon which way one looks at it (and his parents tended to opt for the extravagant formulation, finding their son's expenditures something out of the ordinary) has Proust asking the headwaiter to lend him 50 francs. When Dabescat hands it to him, Proust tells him to keep it, since it was for him all along, and that he will pay him back. A man of absolute honor, Proust never failed to pay anyone back for anything. Liane de Pougy, in her memoirs, speaks of the Ritz, where she found the food mediocre, but the clientele fascinating, and "our charming and faithful Olivier, so sincere and devoted, his affection mingled with his strict sense of etiquette; Olivier, friend and confident of Marcel Proust whose invalid's existence made him depend greatly on gossip and tittle-tattle."

Liane's other reflections vary: "He was always ill, shut away indoors working without cease on the books he has published since then. My friends adored him. His delicate health and his retreat from the world made him seem a rare being in an ivory tower" to an appreciation of his art of listening and telling, when she once met him at Hahn's opera *La Carmélite*, presented at the Opéra Comique: "R[eynaldo], all in a twitter of nerves, had the kind thought of sending Marcel Proust to me in every interval (Proust had departed from custom for this great occasion) to give me his news, collect mine, learn what I was thinking, what my impressions were and those of my entourage. P. brought the notes with a kind smile, transmitted my messages cheerfully . . . He gazed at me with his deep look, his deeply blue look, very gentle and thoughtful. I knew the poetic and melancholy legend which surrounded him . . . a brother-in-suffering to myself." At his demise, she took a more cynical view: "Death of Marcel Proust. We have known forever that he was delicate, and became used to seeing him surviving in spite of it. . . . It has impressed and saddened us. He really did have talent, a strange talent: a sick man's rarified talent which weighed and pondered everything; an elegant talent, above muscular materialism; rather a mannered talent, a bit snobbish, but large, in spite of being diminished by the sick-room. . . . He was clever, loved titled and highly placed people. He was teasing and disdainful, vain and proud of his real importance. With all that, not tremendously sympathetic."

He was also courageous. In his brave waging of a duel with pistols with the ghastly Jean Lorrain, who had maligned him, he felt no fear, he said, just the cold, and they both shot in the air, as was the custom, unlike the duel by sword, in which you had to at least wound your opponent. He once made a note to himself to the effect that homosexuality had never excluded courage, "from Caesar to Kitchener." A further instance exemplified Proust's innate courage. When, at the Ritz there would be air raids, he would keep his calm, comparing the incident in a letter to Mme Straus to a farce by Feydeau, or to El Greco's *Burial of the Count Orgaz*. "Ladies in nightdresses and even in bathrobes roamed through the vaulted lounge, clutching their pearl necklaces to their heart."

The apocalyptic action, celestial and

Giotto di Bondone , The Crucifixion, *1304-1306.*

grounded, would later make him think of Giotto's angels, and, in a time of terrible tragedy, of his beloved Agostinelli's crash into the sea, when he had been taking flying lessons, and had — in a superb irony — given his name as Marcel Swann. In a bizarre moment, Proust, offering Agostinelli an airplane and a Rolls-Royce, both of which were declined, first asked him to cancel the order and then said that he had thought of placing on the side of the airplane he was going to give him the first line of Mallarmé's famous sonnet that Agostinelli so much admired, about the swan who never takes flight: "Le vierge, le vivace et le bel aujourd'hui" (The virgin, lively and lovely today). All very odd.

Perhaps the quotation was meant to refer to not taking flight, but, alas, Agostinelli ignored all the warnings issued, flew out beyond the apprentice flying zone over the Bay of Angels, where he tried to turn without increasing his altitude and was dragged into the sea, too rapidly for the rescue boat to reach him. He sank with all the money Proust had given him, five or six thousand francs.

In the novel, the Narrator will discuss air raids with Saint-Loup, prefacing the tragedy of the fair-haired aristocrat's death in war, and Agostinelli's loss. The reader of the poetry of this epoch may find herself remembering, at this point, Guillaume Apollinaire's epic poem of 1912 entitled "Zone," full of the marvel of airplanes and invoking Christ as the new aviator. Already in his initial travels around the countryside near Cabourg when he had first engaged Agostinelli as his chauffeur, in his bright red taxi, Proust's marveling at the speed of viewing left a mark on his writing as in his mind. "Impressions of the Road from an Automobile," which he wrote for *Le Figaro* and his "Days in an Automobile," in *Contre Sainte-Beuve* describe the steeples of Saint-Etienne as they change their position so rapidly through the car's window, as they speed towards Caen, Agostinelli in his goggles and boots and long coat, an appealing exotic figure. This is of course the model for the Narrator's first written text about the steeples of Martinville from the carriage, in the early days at Combray. In a sense, all of Proust's involvement with Agostinelli — from these early impressions of the countryside speeding along — through the ups and

downs of living with him and his unpleasant wife (about whom
Proust had threatened that he would never help her if anything
were ever to happen to Albert) through the terrible time of his
crash into the sea, has to do with speed and flight. Proust's innate
personal generosity meant, of course, that he did help Anna, the
widow, and his genius of an imagination yielded, from all this and
from Carpaccio and much else, Albertine.

   Proust's marveling at the world and his withdrawal from it are,
in a sense, of a piece.

Leaving Society

The Dreyfus affair split Parisian society apart. Mme Arman's lover, Anatole France, to his everlasting credit, turned in his Legion d'Honneur ribbon when Émile Zola was struck from the rolls because of his stand in favor of Dreyfus: "J'accuse. . . ." went his text, and his accusation sowed dissensions in places expected and less so. Daniel Halévy's Jewish family, to whom Edgar Degas had always been close, saw that great and greatly prejudiced painter leave their house after one dinner in 1897, after not saying a word, never to speak to them again.

Proust, calling himself the first defender of Albert Dreyfus for having taken around a petition in his favor — drawn up by himself and his friends at Mme Straus's — was careful not to offend the other side, and was somehow able to remains friends with the rabid anti-Dreyfusard Léon Daudet and with the "noble and loyal Albu," his friend Louis d'Albufera. Proust was mightily attracted to Albu, who was to be the husband of the actress Louisa de Mornand, and had been first involved with another of Proust's heroes, his adored Bertrand de Fénelon of the "bright blue eyes and flying coattails." With Louisa Proust had a vague flirtation, perhaps in lieu of having it with Albu.

But after years of frequenting salons and dining rooms, and after collecting from his myriad acquaintances the details that would be essential to his work, he grew gradually disillusioned by society's trite superficiality, grew tired of managing, flattering, even entertaining, and turned inward. "We exist alone," he wrote in the *Search*. In a sense, this turn is signaled most significantly by the pages written in 1908-9 in *Against Sainte-Beuve*.
That all-important volume can be read as a long manifesto   *Émile Zola (1840-1902).*

Le Petit Journal

SUPPLÉMENT ILLUSTRÉ

DIMANCHE 20 MARS 1898

LE DUEL HENRY-PICQUART

Above: *The Dreyfus Affair. The duel between Henry and Picquart. Etching by Henri Meyer, for* Le Petit Journal, *March 20, 1898.*

Right: *Émile Zola reading his letter to the jury, during the Dreyfus affair.*

about the originality of genius as opposed to the ordinariness of the rest of human life and involvement with others, including what Proust will finally feel as a waste of time: that is, conversation. The writer who is to write for the universal must use every particular to perfection, but must write and work and live alone. This was finally to be Proust's way.

Always possessed of the perfect excuse of quite extraordinary illness and an even more extraordinary schedule, Proust made his life an art — predicting how long his various reactions to situations would last, requiring his sleep to run from the morning until three in the afternoon, doing his writing and investigating in the night hours, calling upon others to adjust to his requirements. Cecilia Hayward, the agreeable typist from Cabourg whom he hired in 1911, and Albert Nahmias later, were confronted with his reams of almost illegible writing, and subsequently the publishers (Grasset, and then Gallimard) with his meters of proof corrections, Céleste pasting on the reams of pages numerous strips of emendations, branching out from the original like a new sort of tree of creation. Never was there such a massive literary enterprise.

What Proust did not follow through in life could greatly bother him. In 1912, he wrote to Mme Scheikévitch that he was troubled by "any woman in the slightest agreeable, showing her an interest that I can't subsequently sustain."[6] His mother was the only woman to whom he was ever closely attracted, and she died — after a two-year mourning of her husband — on September 26, 1905. In his journal, Reynaldo Hahn describes him grieving by her bed, "weeping and smiling through his tears at her body," prey to the conflicting emotions of love and loss. His life, he wrote Montesquiou, had lost "its only purpose, its only sweetness, its only love, its only consolation."

Proust Abed

Proust's arrangements for living were to be, after the years of society and going out — those of staying in. What he had observed — and every detail of it — gleaned from everyone he encountered, he was then to use. Lying abed, muffled to the neck, always with clean linen, he needed things exactly so, in his "sacred and chaotic bedroom." Céleste Albaret, his housekeeper, nurse, friend, companion, faithful servant — tall and svelte, a surprise to his visitors meeting her for the first time — was precisely what Monsieur Proust most needed. In her memoirs, we find the author at home, in bed and often taking drugs of various kinds to sleep or shut out sounds that somehow penetrated his room: "Veronal, opium, etc. . . . and since I have some albumin, that brings on a thousand ills." Among the other drugs were adrenaline and morphine. And then of course he would take numerous cups of coffee, seventeen at a stretch, to stay awake. Sometimes he would put the drugs in the coffee, mixing Veronal and caffeine. It has been calculated that he spent the equivalent of about $20,000 a year on medication. So doing, he lived to write.

The idea for his cork-lined room came from Anna de Noailles, who had gotten it from the writer Henry Bernstein. Proust had had a feather comforter made at Liberty's of London, but this was exceptionally bad for an asthma sufferer, who had to fumigate himself, by his reckoning, up to six hours a day with Legras powders, and who, when he was in company, smoked Espic anti-asthma cigarettes. When he was in bed, the candle would always be ready for this, and the square of paper with which to light the powder. His fur coat would be placed over his feet, hanging down the side of the bed, and a black raincoat would be ready at the bottom of the bed. Céleste would prepare his hot water bottles, for he was always cold, to the point of insisting, wherever he went for dinner — to the Ritz or to some grand hostess — that all the windows must be closed and the room kept at a certain temperature: 86° Fahrenheit.

Before him stood his tables, one with notebooks and a moleskin pad, one with the silver platter and the coffeepot that would be exchanged at night for a lacquer platter with lime tea and Evian water. A little stack of white linen towels would be present, and hooks to hang his clothes on, which he never used. Between the windows, before the chest of drawers stood a grand piano for Reynaldo Hahn to play — his constant friend, who watched over him even at the hour of his death. No one was closer to him longer, and Proust's letters to Hahn, with their witty illustrations, are among the richest sources for biographers.

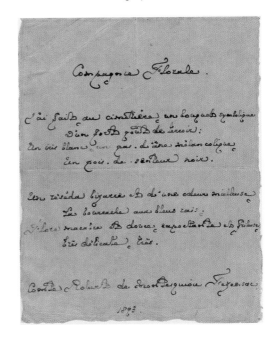

*"The Company of Flowers"
("Compagnie Florale"), a
poem by Count Robert de
Montesquiou.*

Inexplicable Proust

Many things in Proust's life strike us as wonderfully odd. For example, Proust's pastiches and parodies were often signed with other names. One such occasion already mentioned, was his writing of an evening at Montesquiou's, signed "Horatio," which so appealed to the Fatal Count that he memorized it, recited it everywhere, and circulated it for a few friends, after making a "few necessary changes." Queried as to whether he wrote it, Proust of course denied it . . . until later, when Montesquiou could not protest, having first welcomed it.

Then there was the time in which, in order to test his friendship, he wrote Fénelon a letter signed Bibesco in which he says that he no longer feels any friendship for Marcel, who is even stupider than before. Genius has most surely its more peculiar sides.

It is perhaps his inexplicable bursts of emotion that strike the most responsive chord in many of us. Marie Nordlinger, describing what it was like to work with him on the Ruskin translations, speaks of his omnivorous memory. He would have memorized all the dictionary definitions of any word or expression troubling him, as well as all of his favorite books by Ruskin: *Praeterita* (whose title, *Times Past*, is not unlike that of his own project) and the others, and his way of listening: "interrogating, probing with his strangely luminous, omnivorous eyes. Eyes I can recall alight with fun and mimicry or suddenly suffused unaccountably, unashamedly, with tears."[7] At the home of the poet Anna de Noailles, he made some extravagant gesture and swept her most precious Tanagra figurine to the floor. He would replace it before feeling he could return — it took him a year — but in the meantime she had saved the pieces, as a relic of his gesture.

His actions could be rather strange. With a burst of anger at some insult Fénelon proffered, he proceeded to flail him with his fists and then stamped on the hat he had just purchased for a trip, tore it apart and ripped out its lining. When in the novel, Charlus makes the same gesture, we are suddenly aware that the correspondence between text and life is as close in the Narrator/Marcel's own case as in that of his characters. It often feels as if he were working out his writing in his life, as frequently as the reverse: there are often two ways in Proust.

Knowing the Ending

One of the last dinners Proust attended was given at the Ritz by the Sydney Schiffs. It included James Joyce — they had not read each other's work, too busy writing their own, and mutually complained only of their headaches and digestion — and Diaghilev, whom Proust had known so long ago, when his Ballets Russes first came to Paris. His visitors included his friend from long ago, Lucien Daudet, and his more recent friend, the blond and child-faced diplomat Paul Morand. Morand was the future husband of the Princess Soutzo, with whom Proust had so often come out of his reclusivity to dine in the Ritz, on lobster and champagne, the cost of which he shared, occasioning, as did his other extravagances, much the concern of his stockbroker, Lionel Hauser. The latter finally resigned, but left Proust's finances in good shape, in spite of all his expenditures.

Towards the end, when Proust had gone again to see the Vermeer and had then fallen in his room, he had difficulty speaking. What he wanted more than anything was to finish his books. Gallimard wanted to bring out a *Selected Writings*, which Proust was all in favor of, but events then went too

James Joyce (1882-1941), Irish writer, in France, around 1930.

quickly. A pharmacist had mislabeled a prescription of Veronal, so he had taken too much. He continued to go out to dinners at Mme Soutzo's and to preserve his contact with the Sydney Schiffs. It was increasingly an effort to eat and to keep warm: he would survive on Vichy water, potatoes, croissants, and noodles, constantly wondering if it was warmer in the kitchen. Now he thought of himself, as he said to the Schiffs, as a "misshapen and staggering thing" when he had to go to a book signing. Directly after that, he went home with a raging fever, and from then on, consumed only ice cream and icy beer from the Ritz. He felt his death was hastened by a fire in his chimney, and by leaving his bed in cold weather in a vain attempt to see Ernest Forssgren, who had sent him a note from his hotel, and then not returned before Proust, exhausted and freezing, had given up in despair and gone home. He was also dogged by a fear that Montesquiou would have attacked him in his memoirs (*Les Pas effacés*/ "Footsteps Rubbed Out"), to be posthumously published. He asked Edmond Jaloux, charged with editing them, to remove his name completely from the text. Sadly, Proust died unaware of how fortunate he was to have had Charles Kenneth Scott Montcrieff as his first real translator.

After a series of coughing fits, and a final cold and bronchitis and pneumonia, he succumbed, having refused to take the medication prescribed by Dr. Bize. At the end, the doctor at Proust's bedside, called by Céleste, and at her urging, gave him an injection which Proust had not wanted: "Céleste, oh Céleste," he cried. She was stricken with guilt, having only wanted to save him. Robert, by his side, reassured her she had done as she had thought best.

The witty and humble Abbé Mugnier, Proust's favourite priest, whom he had so wanted to pray at last by his bedside, was too ill to come. But every year after, he held a memorial in Proust's honor. It was this priest that Proust had teased: "Do you know the *Fleurs du mal*, Father?" "Yes," said the Abbé, patting his shabby soutane from beneath which his old square-toed shoes protruded, "I carry it here always. If we didn't know about sin, how could we recognize virtue?" And recognize it he had, in Proust.

Left: Rembrandt (1606-1669),
Self-portrait at the Age of Sixty-three,
1669.

Below: *Marcel Proust*
on his deathbed.

For it was, of course, Proust's *In Search of Lost Time* that had saved him forever, when that time proved never to have been wasted, and never to have completely gone. At the funeral, bundled up, there was James Joyce, come to pay his respects to a writer he had at last acknowledged as his equal. The scene might remind us of one imagined by Proust so much earlier, when Rembrandt is sitting enthroned as the king of painting, and an old man hobbles in, before whom the crowds part as he makes his way toward the throne and the two masters meet. It is John Ruskin, whose words Proust so often invoked, placing beside them the words from a bible on which the English master's *Bible of Amiens* was based. Translator and writer, Frenchman and Englishman, agreed on them: "Work, for the night cometh when no man can work."

Yet it may well be, as Proust had said, that "the part of ourselves that matters, when it matters, is outside time."[8]

References

1. Quoted by Proust in a letter to Antoine Bibesco, July, 1904.
2. Fernand Gregh, *Cahiers Marcel Proust*, 1, pp. 35-6.
3. To Marie Nordlinger, February, 1904.
4. To Léon Yeatman, August 1904.
5. Cocteau, *Journal*, January 1945, p. 615.
6. To Madame Scheikévitch, September 7, 1912.
7. Marie Nordlinger, *Proust and Ruskin*, exhibition catalog, Whitworth Gallery, Manchester University, pp. 9-10.
8. Letter to Lucien Daudet.

Chronology

1871   Marcel Proust born to Jeanne Weil Proust (1849-1905, from a Parisian-Jewish family), and Professeur Adrien Proust (1834-1903, a grocer's son, from a Catholic family), in Auteuil, during the Paris Commune; baptized August 5, at St.-Louis d'Antin.

1873   Birth of Proust's brother, Robert. Both children are raised as Catholics, although the parents are not practicing church-goers. August, the family moves to 9, boulevard Malesherbes.

1882-89   Attends Lycée Condorcet, on the rue Caumartin, where Paul Desjardins (founder of the décades at Pontigny) and Alphonse Darlu, the philosopher, are his professors in the last years. Marcel writes for school magazines (*Le Lundi, La Revue Lilas*), with his schoolmates Daniel Halévy, Fernand Gregh, Robert Dreyfus, Louis de La Salle, Robert de Flers, and Jacques Bizet, whose mother, Geneviève, becomes one of Proust's great friends. In her apartment at 22, rue de Douai, he meets many artists and musicians.

1886   Meets Marie Benardaky; after Bizet's death, Geneviève becomes Mme Emile Straus, in whose salon on the boulevard Haussmann Proust meets Sarah Bernhardt, Gabriel Fauré, Guy de Maupassant, Edgar Degas, the Princesse Mathilde, and Charles Haas, a Jew accepted in society (the Cercle de la rue Royale and the Jockey

Club), who will be the principal source for Swann in Proust's novel.

1889   November, joins 76th Infantry Régiment in Orléans; the family pays for his soldier's uniform, enabling a short stay in the army.

1890   January, Proust's Grandmother, Mme Nathé Weil, dies; November, he attends the Sorbonne as a law student.

1892   Publishes in *Le Banquet*.

1893   Publishes in *La Revue blanche* (celebrated Symbolist journal: associated with Thadée Natanson, Misia Sert, Stéphane Mallarmé, Edouard Vuillard, among others); meets Comte Robert de Montesquiou-Fezensac.

1895   Receives Philosophy degree.

1895-1900 On staff of Mazarine Library; travels widely in Europe.

1896   Proust's great-uncle, Louis Weil, dies in Auteuil; June, *Les Plaisirs et les jours* is published.

1897   Duels with Jean Lorrain.

1898   Circulates a petition for revision of Dreyfus decision.

1900   Publishes articles on Ruskin; May, travels to Padua and Venice; family moves to 45, rue de Courcelles.

1902   October, travels in Belgium and Holland.

1903   Robert marries; November, Proust's father dies.

1904   Proust's translation of Ruskin's *Bible of Amiens* is published.

1905   September, Proust's mother dies; December, is admited to Dr. Sollier's nursing home, suffering from nervous disorders (leaves in January 1906).

1906	Publication of Proust's translation of Ruskin's *Sesame and Lilies*; moves into 102, Boulevard Haussmann.
1907	Vacations at Cabourg; employs Alfred Agostinelli as his chauffeur.
1908	Completes draft of the novel; first volume is published in 1913.
1910	Installs cork lining in his bedroom, while in Cabourg.
1912	First version of *À la recherche* revised, typed; Agostinelli becomes his live-in secretary; excerpts published in *Le Figaro*; novel rejected by André Gide at the *Nouvelle Revue Français* and by Fasquelle.
1913	Novel rejected by Ollendorf; March, accepted by Grasset, with Proust paying for publication; November, *Du côté de chez Swann* published.
1914	May, Agostinelli killed in his plane, despite warnings; June, July, publication in the *NRF* of excerpts from *Le côté de Guermantes*.
1916	*NRF* takes over from Grasset as Proust's publisher.
1918	February, meets Hélène (Chrissoveloni) Soutzo (wife of Dimitri Soutzo-Doudesco), who will marry Proust's friend Paul Morand, and frequents the Ritz Hotel, where she lives.
1919	Has to leave Boulevard Haussmann (the building will become a bank); stays in house of the actress Réjane (Gabrielle Réju) on the rue Laurent-Pichat; Moves into 44, rue Hamelin; *A l'ombre des jeunes filles en fleurs* published; *Pastiches et mélanges* published; *Du côté de chez Swann* reissued; December, *A l'ombre des jeunes filles en fleurs* awarded the Prix Goncourt.

1920	Receives the Légion d'honneur; *Le côté de Guermantes I* published; *Le côté de Guermantes II* and *Sodome et Gomorrhe I* published; Montesquiou-Fezensac dies.
1922	*Sodome et Gomorrhe II* published; November 18, Proust dies in Paris.
1923	*La Prisonnière* published.
1925	*Albertine disparue* published.
1927	*Le Temps retrouvé* published.

Bibliography

Marcel Proust *À la recherche du temps perdu,* Paris: Gallimard, Bibliothèque de la Pléiade, 4 vols, 1987-9.

Marcel Proust, *Correspondance Générale,* publiée par Robert Proust et Paul Brach, La Palatine: A la Librairie Plon, 1935.

Marcel Proust, *Correspondence*, ed. Philip Kolb, Paris: Plon, 1970-93, 21 vols.

Marcel Proust, *In Search of Lost Time,* tr. C.K. Scott Moncrieff and Terence Kilmartin, and by Andreas Mayor, revised by D.J. Enright, 6 vols. London: Chatto & Windus, 1992.

Marcel Proust, *In Search of Lost Time,* ed. Christopher Prendergast. London: Penguin, 2002; New York: Penguin UK and US, 2003.

Marcel Proust, *Selected Letters.* (5 vol.) Edited by Philip Kolb, translated by Terence Kilmartin. New York: Oxford University Press, 1989.

Marcel Proust, l'écriture et les arts, catalogue to the Bibliothèque Nationale exhibition, ed. Jean-Yves Tadié, Gallimard/BNF, 1999.

Céleste Albaret, *Monsieur Proust: Souvenirs Recueillis par Georges Belmont.* Paris: Robert Laffont, 1973; Tr. Barbara Bray, Harvill, 1976.

Samuel Beckett, *Proust.* London: Chatto & Windus, 1931; New York: Grove, 1931.

Alain de Botton, *How Proust Can Change Your Life*. London: Picador, 1997; New York: Pantheon, 1997.

Malcolm Bowie, *Proust Among the Stars.* London: HarperCollins, 1998; New York: Columbia University Press, 1998.

Brassai, *Marcel Proust sous l'emprise de la photographie*.Paris: Gallimard, 1997.

William C. Carter, *Marcel Proust: A Life*. New Haven: Yale University Press, 2000.

Mary Ann Caws and Eugène Nicole, *Reading Proust Now*. New York: Peter Lang, 1990.

Jean Cocteau, *Journal: 1942-1945*. Paris: Gallimard, Texte établi, annoté et presenté par Jean Touzot.

Colette, *Pays connu*. (Paris: 1950) New York: Columbia, 1998.

Mina Curtiss, *Other People's Letters*. Boston: Houghton Mifflin, 1978.

Lynn Garafola and Nancy Van Norman Baer, *The Ballets Russes and its World*. 1999.

Reynaldo Hahn, *Notes. Journal d'un musicien*, Plon: 1933.

Paul Magriel, *Nijinsky*. New York: Henry Holt, 1946.

Ronald Hayman, *Proust*. Minerva. London: Heinemann, 1990; Minerva paperback, 1991.

Robert de Montesquiou, *Marcel Proust*. Paris: 1925.

Robert de Montesquiou, *Ou l'art de paraître*. Paris: Réunion des musées nationaux, 1999.

Paul Nadar, *Le Monde de Proust: Souvenir: Period photographs by Paul Nadar*. London: 1984; *Le Monde de Proust, vu par Paul Nadar*. Paris: Éditions du patrimoine, 1999; English edition, Cambridge: MIT Press, 2002.

Marie Nordlinger, *Proust and Ruskin*. Manchester: Whitworth Gallery.

George D. Painter, *Marcel Proust: A Biography*. London: Random House, 1959, revised and enlarged edition, London: Chatto & Windus, 1989; George D. Painter, *Marcel Proust: A Biography*, revised edition. London: Pimlico, 1996.

Jérôme Picon, *Passion Proust: L'album d'une vie*. Bergamo: Grafedit, 1999.

Liane de Pougy, *My Blue Notebooks: The Intimate Journal of Paris's Most Beautiful and Notorious Courtesan*. New York: Putnam, 2002; Harper, 1979 tr. Diana Athill From *Mes cahiers bleus*, Plon, 1977.

Frank W.D. Ries, *The Dance Theatre of Jean Cocteau*. UMI Research Press, 1986.

William Sansom, *Proust and His World*. London: Thames & Hudson, 1973.

Charles Spencer, *The World of Serge Diaghilev*. Chicago: Henry Regnery Company, 1974.

Yves Tadié, *Marcel Proust: A Life*. Tr. Ewan Cameron. London: Penguin; New York: Viking, 2000.

Edmund White, *Proust*. London: Weidenfeld & Nicolson, 1999; New York: Penguin, 1999.

List of Illustrations

List of illustrations (by page number) and photographic acknowledgments. Every effort has been made to contact all copyright holders. The publisher will be happy to correct in future editions any errors or omissions brought to their attention.

15. (*left*) Vittore Carpaccio, *Legend of St. Ursula, a Christian Princess of Brittany*, 1494. Canvas, 274 x 267 cm. (Copyright Erich Lessing/Art Resource, N.Y.; Accademia, Venice, Italy)

15. (*right*) Dresses of Mariano Fortuny y Madrazo. (Roger Viollet)

16. Marie Benardaky by Paul Nadar, November 30, 1893. (© Centre des monuments nationaux)

17. Count Robert de Montesquiou-Fezensac. (Photo: Franck Raux. Copyright, Réunion des Musees Nationaux/Art Resource, N.Y./Musée d'Orsay, Paris, France)

18. Jean Lorrain, Jean-Louis Forain, fourth from the left, and Robert de Montesquiou-Fezensac. Caricature by Sem. (Bibliothèque nationale, Prints. Roger Viollet)

19. Joseph Mallord William Turner, *Landscape with a River and a Bay in the in Far Distance*. (Copyright Erich Lessing/Art Resource, N.Y/Louvre, Paris.)

21. Poem by Proust: "Si le bleu de l'opale est tendre/ If the blue of the opal is tender..." (Rare Book and Special Collections Library, University of Illinois)

23. The writer Colette, as a "little faun." (Roger Viollet)

24. Élisabeth de Gramont, the Duchesse de Clermont-Tonnerre by Paul Nadar, June 12, 1889. (© Centre des monuments nationaux)

25. Proust at the feet of Jeanne Pouquet, at the tennis court on boulevard Bineau. (Bibliothèque nationale de France.)

27. Marcel Proust by Jacques-Émile Blanche. (Beinecke Library, Yale University/Musée d'Orsay, Paris, France)

29. The Grand Hotel, in Cabourg (Calvados), ca. 1900. (Roger Viollet.)

31. Fragment of manuscript by Proust. (Rare Book and Special Collections Library, University of Illinois)

33. Restaurant Larue, Paris, in 1938. (Roger Viollet)

34. Madame Georges Aubernon by Paul Nadar, January 18, 1883 (Centre des monuments nationaux)

35. The Countess Greffulhe by Paul Nadar, 1896. (© Centre des monuments nationaux)

36. Laure Hayman by Paul Nadar, November 25, 1879. (© Centre des monuments nationaux)

37. Sarah Bernhardt by Georges Clairin. 1876. Oil on canvas, 250 X 200 cm. (Photo: Bulloz. Musée du Petit Palais, Paris. Roger Viollet)

38. (*left*) Charles Haas by Paul Nadar, December 26, 1895. (© Centre des monuments nationaux)

38. (*right*) Jockey Club in Chantilly (Oise), 1909. (Roger Viollet)

39. Reynaldo Hahn by Paul Nadar, 1898. (© Centre des monuments nationaux)

40. Oscar Wilde. (Roger Viollet)

41. Gustave Moreau, *The Apparition*, ca. 1876. Watercolor 412 x 28 $^{3/8}$ in. (photo: J.G. Berizzi. Copyright Réunion des Musées Nationaux /Art Resource, N.Y./Louvre, Paris, France)

42. (*top*) Gaston Calmette by Paul Nadar, 1899. (© Centre des monuments nationaux)

42. (*right*) Letter from Marcel Proust to Gaston Calmette. (Beinecke Library, Yale)

43. André Gide, at his piano in the rue Vaneau, Paris. (Roger Viollet)

45. James Abbott McNeill Whistler, *Harmony in Blue and Silver*. Trouville, 1845. (Copyright Erich Lessing/Art Resource, N.Y./Isabella Stewart Gardner Museum, Boston)

46. Portrait of Count Robert de Montsquiou by James Abbott McNeill Whistler. (Frick Museum, New York)

47. (*top*) Stéphane Mallarmé with Auguste Renoir, on the sofa by Edgar Degas.

47. (*bottom*) James Abbott McNeill Whistler, *Arrangement in Grey and Black No. 2*, or the *Artist's Mother* (Anna Mathilda McNeill, 1804-81), Oil on canvas, 1871. (Copyright Erich Lessing/Art Resource, N.Y./Museé d'Orsay, Paris, France)

49. (*top*) The Marquis de Castellane. (Roger Viollet)

49. (*bottom*) Giovanni Boldini, *Count Robert de Montesquiou*. 1897. Oil on canvas., 160 x 82.5. (Photo: Herve Lewandowski. Copyright Réunion des Musées Nationaux/Art Resource, N.Y.Musée d'Orsay, Paris, France.)

50. (*top*) Sarah Bernhardt in Racine's *Phèdre* by Paul Nadar, 1893. (© Centre des monuments nationaux)

50. (*bottom*) La comtesse Anna de Noailles. (Roger Viollet)

51. (*top*) Natalie Clifford Barney. (Roger Viollet)

51. (*bottom*) Liane de Pougy. (Roger Viollet)

52. Poster for Jean Lorrain and Ed. Diet, "Rêve de Noël," performed by Liane de Pougy and Rose Demay at the Olympia, in December of 1896, in Paris. (Roger Viollet)

54. Sarah Bernhardt, by Paul Nadar. (Copyright Réunion des Musées Nationaux/Art Resource, N.Y./Musée d'Orsay, Paris)

55. John Ruskin, *Self-Portrait in Blue Neckcloth*. Watercolor. (Art Resource/J. Pierpont Morgan Library, Gift of the Fellows, 1959)

56. Article by Proust, from the *Gazette des Beaux-Arts*, with manuscript corrections. (Rare Book and Special Collections Library, University of Illinois)

57. Contract with the *Mercure de France*, for translation of Ruskin's *La Bible d'Amiens*. February 26, 1904. (Rare Book and Special Collections Library, University of Illinois)

58. James Abbott McNeill Whistler, *Nocturne in Blue and Silver: Chelsea*, 1871. (Art Resource/Tate Gallery, London, England)

59. Stéphane Mallarmé and Méry Laurent by Paul Nadar, February 26, 1896. (© Centre des monuments nationaux)

61. Willie Heath by Paul Nadar, June 28, 1883. (© Centre des monuments nationaux)

63. Jan Vermeer, *View of Delft,* ca, 1658. (Copyright Scala/Art Resouce, N.Y./Mauritshuis, The Hague, The Netherlands)

64. (*above left*) Jean-Baptiste Simeon Chardin, *Self-Portait at his Easel*, pastel color. 1776. (Photo: J.G.Berizzi. Copyright Réunion des Musées Nationaux/Art Resource, N.Y. Musée d'Orsay, Paris)

64. (*above right*) Jean-Baptiste Simeon Chardin, *The Buffet*. Oil on canvas. (Photo: J.G. Berizzi/ Copyright Réunion des Musées Nationaux/Art Resource, N.Y./Musée du Louvre, Paris)

64. (*below*) Édouard Manet, *Olympia*. 1863. Oil on canvas. (Photo: Hervé Lewandowski. Copyright Réunion des Museés Nationaux/Art Resource, N.Y./Musée d'Orsay, Paris)

65. Jean Antoine Watteau. *The Embarkation for Cythera*. Oil on canvas, 129 x 194 cm. (Photo: Gérard Blot. Coypright Rénion des Musées Nationaux/Art Resource, N.Y./Musée du Louvre, Paris)

66. (*top*) Vittore Carpaccio, *The Meeting of the Betrothed Couple and the Departure of the Pilgrims*, from the *Legend of Saint Ursula*, 1495. 280 x 611 cm. (Copyright Alinari/Art Resource, N.Y./Accademia, Venice, Italy)

66. (*bottom*) Claude Monet, *Cathedral of Rouen, Portal and Tour Saint-Romain, Harmony in Blue and Gold*. 1894. oil on canvas, 107 x 73 cm. (Photo: Hervé Lewandowski. Copyright Réunion des Musées Nationaux/Art Resource, N.Y/Musée d'Orsay Paris)

67. Décor for Claude Debussy's *Pelléas et Mélisande*, by L. Jusseaume. First set, 1902. (Musée des arts Décoratifs. Roger Viollet)

68-69. Pastiche of Pelléas. (Rare Book and Special Collections Library, University of Illinois)

69. Sarah Bernhardt, in the role of Pelléas in *Pelléas et Mélisande* by Maurice Maeterlinck, London, 1907. (Paris: Bibliothèque de l'Arsenal. Roger Viollet)

70. (*top*) Ad for the "Théâtrophone." (Roger Viollet)

70. (*bottom*) and **71** (*top*) Pelléas et Mélisande, score: "Je respire enfin..." (New York Public Library: Music Division)

72. (*top*) Reynaldo Hahn, music set to a poem by Paul Verlaine. (New York Public Library, Music Division)

72. (*bottom*) César Franck: Sonata in A Major for Piano and Violin. (New York Public Library, Music Division)

73. (*top*) Saint-Saëns, Sonata opus 75, for piano and violin, in D minor, 1885. (New York Public Library, Music Division)

73. (*bottom*) Wagner, prelude from *Parsifal*. (New York Public Library, Music Division)

74. *Portrait of Sergei Diaghilev* by Jean Cocteau. (Copyright ARS, N.Y., drawn posthumously in 1954. Copyright Snark/Art Resource, N.Y.)

75. Nijinsky as the Golden Slave in Diaghilev's *Schéhérazade*.

77. (*top*) Édouard Manet, *The Asparagus*, 1880. (Copyright Scala/Art Resource N.Y. Musée d'Orsay, Paris)